BREAKING THROUGH & REACHING OUT

VOLUME 1: A Call to Engage – Enjoying the Presence

by
Gordon Campbell

Kingdom Publishers

Breaking Through and Reaching Out

VOLUME 1: A Call to Engage – Enjoying the Presence

Copyright© Gordon Campbell

All rights reserved. No part of this book may be reproduced in any form by photocopying or any electronic or mechanical means, including information storage or retrieval systems, without permission in writing from both the copyright owner and the publisher of the book. The right of Gordon Campbell to be identified as the author of this work has been asserted by him in accordance with the Copyright, Designs and Patents Act 1988 and any subsequent amendments thereto.

A catalogue record for this book is available from the British Library.

All Scripture Quotations have been taken from the New International Version of the Bible.

ISBN: 978-1911697-37-4

1st Edition by Kingdom Publishers

Kingdom Publishers
London, UK.

You can purchase copies of this book from any leading bookstore or email

contact@kingdompublishers.co.uk

Dedication

To my parents the Reverend Joseph and Barbara Campbell (both deceased), my wife Gillian Campbell , my children, in-laws and young grandchildren who have been prayerfully supportive throughout my journey.

Explanation

To be driven to write a book comes with a health warning, because no author knows how a published work will appeal to the public nor how it will sell. Initially, the intention was to write one book, but after consultation the one book has become two. The main title: Breaking Through and Reaching Out retains its place, but is now in two volumes:

Book 1 is subtitled: A Call to Engage – Enjoying the Presence

Book 2 is subtitled: A Call to Ignite – Living in the Spirit

Each of the two volumes contains four parts covering a variety of topics but the parts contain progression from one part to the next part, although each part is singular in that each theme is self-authenticating.

The normal practice when reading books is to start from the front and read through until reaching the final page. You can certainly do that, but you may find that there is another way you may be attuned towards. There are those who are addicted to reading the last chapter of a book first, then review the rest of the book. They take the view that very often the punch-lines are to be found in the closing sections of the book, which they find stimulating. My style is such that the parts do over run each other in certain areas to cement the values of each part, but where they are repeated remind the reader of the previous sections. I hope you find this explanation helpful, if not just read the books using your own inimitable approach.

Book 1:

A Call to Engage – Enjoying the Presence

Acknowledgements

- *Grateful thanks ...*
- *to the theological seminaries of Cliff College, Spurgeon's College and London, Brunel and Middlesex Universities, where I learned so much from interactive learning;*
- *to the pastoral teachers who opened my eyes to the world of learning, particularly Cyril Chilvers, Don English, George Beasley-Murray, Raymond Brown, and David Pytches;*
- *to the Baptist churches I have had the privilege of serving in London, Portsmouth, Harrow, and Dulwich - for the part they played in stimulating me to pursue our journey together for his glory;*
- *to CNEC (now World Share) for my role as honorary Director for ten years, during which time I met church leaders from around the world across four continents;*
- *to the mission conferences I attended in Canada, the United States and Brazil, which gave me a global perspective on what God was doing among many different nations, cultures and peoples;*
- *to the partnership teams I engaged with in the UK and the USA, that proved invaluable 'testing grounds' for missional teaching, learning and faith sharing in local churches.*
- *to the colleagues I served with on the ministry teams at the New Wine summer conferences at Shepton Mallet and Newark;*
- *to the many colleagues in pastoral ministry who were inspirational in forming my understanding, thinking and experience in the Gospel, the Kingdom, the Word and Spirit, which became such vital ingredients for my pastoral ministry;*
- *to the staff and students of Bushey Meads Secondary Academy School, where I was Head of Religious Education and Pastoral Head of Year for twelve years, who earthed me into the realities of daily life;*

- *to the many writers whose theological, biblical and spiritual writings gave me considerable pleasure and inspired me to integrate evangelical and charismatic beliefs and practices*
- *and most of all to my parents and my wife Gill who along with members of my family, for their constant love, support, and encouragement with the words, 'get the work done.'*
- *I thank Pastor Malcolm Hathaway for kindly providing the foreword.*

Contents

Dedication 3

Explanation 5

Acknowledgements 9

Foreword 13

Endorsements: 14

Prologue 17

Preface 20

PART 1 Releasing the Kingdom - Today 25

PART 2 Celebrating the Spirit's Ministry – in the Gospels 70

PART 3 Water and Spirit – a Glorious Event 108

PART 4 Living and Dying – Identity 151

Appendices: Shaping the Future - Stoking the Fire;
    The Foundational Basis of Dynamic Prayer Ministry ... 186

Bibliography 205

Foreword

It's not surprising that the men Jesus called to be his disciples didn't know how to pray. Some of them were tough young fishermen, eking out an existence on the Sea of Galilee to support their families. One a tax collector, collaborating with the puppet king Herod. These were men of the world, not given to a lot of prayer. So as they observed Jesus praying they asked him 'Lord, teach us to pray'. The prayer Jesus taught them that day, and teaches every disciple today is not a set form of words, but a pattern for prayer.

Growing up in the 60's the Lord's Prayer was said each day at morning assembly in my school. Known universally as a set prayer, for most it is not really prayer - more like grace before a meal. Thanks for your daily bread. Not many even do that any more! What Jesus taught as a pattern for prayer is that after opening worship the first plea is 'Your Kingdom Come, Your will be done on earth as in heaven'. The end of the set prayer today is 'Yours is the kingdom...' Doesn't take a lot to realise the importance of the Kingdom to Jesus. He is the King!

How wonderful to be able to read so much more about the life-changing meaning of the Kingdom of God. What it means to today's disciples. How it should shape our daily lives, our families, our churches, our community. To be led by thoughtful study and reflection, spiced with quotations from God's Word and distilled from so many teachers and preachers. To discover how to break through and reach out for the King! The story of the Kingdom of God!

Enjoy your journey of exploration and discovery with Gordon Campbell!

Rev Malcolm Hathaway BD,

Pastor and teacher

Endorsements:

I have known Gordon Campbell for more than 50 years. He was my pastor when I was a theological student in London. One is left in no doubt as to his deep spiritual convictions and commitment to the values of God's kingdom. This came through very clearly in his preaching and now in these two volumes which tell us of his personal story, but also of his vision of a world made new by God's spirit.

The central issue of this book is the kingdom or rule of God. Though Christianity and the church appear to be in decline to the point of extinction, this is not the case, and neither can it be the case. God has promised to preserve his church from all the forces of opposition and previews the incoming of a new earth and a new heaven. Campbell is both an optimist and a realist. He accepts that the world has turned its back on God, but at the same time makes it clear that God has not abandoned the church as a force for good. This book explains how God embraces the world as he indwells the church and will fulfil his purposes for both.

Dr John Dyer, Baptist minister, former missionary in Brazil, writer, and Coordinator of the Timothy Project.

Christianity is the best news the world has ever heard. It focuses on the hope for eternal life and resurrection, made possible through the life, death and resurrection of Jesus Christ. The joy of the gospel comes from knowing Jesus, God's Anointed.

In order to enjoy the Presence of the living God, however, you must first fully engage with God's Word and the claims of faith.

Produced over two volumes, Gordon Campbell enables the reader to do just that; to start over by reassessing the claims of faith, by looking once again at the model of the Early Church and how it became a dynamic force that changed the world by living out the Good News of Jesus.

In every age, Christians are called not just to be 'hearers' of the gospel but 'doers'.

Today, the church is a sleeping giant and the task of re-engaging both believer and non-believer is a daunting challenge but one that the author sets about in Breaking Through and Reaching Out, with great enthusiasm.

I would recommend this book to anyone who wants to reconnect to the Source of life or has lost their way or who feels distant from the Kingdom of God.

Rev. Norman Nicoll

I have known Gordon for almost 3 decades and have come to value his breadth of knowledge, experience and conviction. His bi-vocational background in Christian ministry and Religious Education has given him a unique profile. On the one hand he has a capacity to 'catch the breeze' of new spiritual movements within the church without loosing his hold on its orthodox faith, and on the other his secular work in education has not allowed him to escape the scrutiny of competing worldviews. This profile gives Gordon a capacity to offer wise observations in both spheres.

The two volumes offer the reader an opportunity to engage with Gordons distilled wisdom drawn from diverse contexts and fuelled by an evangelical desire to see the church grow and flourish. C S Lewis once wrote that "Most people don't need to be taught, they need only to be reminded." Gordon does this admirably and his work merits reading as it urges us, once more, to 'live by the Spirit'.

Rev Chris Casey BA(Hons), PGCE
Area Dean of Burnley/Interim Area Dean of Pendle Vicar of St John the Divine, Cliviger with St John the Evangelist, Worsthorne

As we look at the world in which we live, we see the pace of change accelerating and the nature of change rapidly evolving. The increasing volatility, uncertainty, complexity and ambiguity that we experience requires us to think deeply about our response as Christians. In this book, Gordon Campbell rightly challenges us to examine our calling as a Kingdom community that both models a better way and seeks to bring transformation and hope to the world around it. Gordon's commitment to the word and Spirit will cause you to ask many important questions and consider what it means to, "... belong to God, but live in a foreign land."

Revd Rich Webb, MEng, MA (Cantab), MTh

I have known the author for over fifty years, and he brings his impressive experience as a pastor and teacher to address the biblical theme of the Kingdom of God. It is a grand theme too often neglected, but the author is persuasive in his challenge to the Church to fully partake in the lifestyle of the kingdom. Earthly kingdoms serve to delude and deceive us, and only God's kingdom has transforming power. The followers of Jesus should constantly renew their calling as ambassadors of the new kingdom God is bringing to birth through Christ. Study this book and it will stir a longing to experience the power and joy of God's gracious Kingdom.

David Coffey OBE
Past President of the Baptist World Alliance
Former General Secretary of the Baptist Union of Great Britain.

Prologue

A Story

Anyone who comes from Glasgow comes with baggage, tends to emerge with an optimistic or pessimistic view of life. Somehow I found myself stuck in the middle unlike some of my contemporaries. This middle-ground determined how I pictured life and that trend has continued with me throughout life. That factor was evidenced in my early church connections which gave me a varied ecclesiology. My parents, ardent Christians, attended four different churches – not at the same time, of course. Their main commitment was to a mission in the centre of Glasgow. It was in one of the poorest areas of the city with poverty, a high crime rate and inadequate housing. Despite the downside, the mission was the main community of faith we attended, and I loved the atmosphere. I have a vivid memory of a black pastor and singers from the southern States of the USA, holding a month's evangelistic mission in downtown Glasgow. Their approach was to preach, sings gospel songs, tell stories and play their band of 'silver instruments' to trumpet the message. For people in the area it was a bit of heaven on earth, and I loved it.

    The mission was held in the Tent Hall, sited amid high rise flats populated by people from many deprived backgrounds. The name of the auditorium, which could hold more than 2,000 people at the Saturday/Sunday events, arose out of the D.L. Moody evangelistic crusades in the late 19th century. Moody had preached on Glasgow Green, a vast park, and had used a Tent to shelter people from the inclement weather. Many thousands responded to the gospel, but the churches were unable to cope with the numbers because there was a cultural gulf between the church and the people. Thankfully, Christian businessmen bought a building in Salt Street which they named the Tent Hall, after Moody's tent, for 'gospel' work. Sadly, that mission is no longer there for in its place stands a huge Mosque (Masjid – Arabic) purchased by Saudi Arabian money. Such a dramatic contrast is contrary to the motto of the city by St Mungo (6th c) which, in full, declares: 'Let Glasgow flourish by the preaching of his word and the praising of his name.' The Tent Hall may be gone, but the gospel is now trumpeted across the city by a growing number of Gospel kingdom churches.

My time in Glasgow came to a dramatic end when my father, having accepted the call to be pastor of a Messianic Church in Stamford Hill, London. In the city, I entered into a completely new world. It wasn't only that Londoners were different from what I had been used to, many of the people who were members of the church had survived the Holocaust in Europe. As a non-Jewish family (Goyem, Gentiles) our background was different, but they were loving, warm and friendly to us, and soon introduced us to songs and prayers in Hebrew, Polish and English. Five years later, my father received a call to a Baptist Church on Tyneside, and I became an adopted 'Geordie.' The community was sizeable, with several hundred members and over a thousand young people. The way of doing church in these last two 'churches,' was distinctly different from what I had been used to in Scotland. Somehow, I emerged from these conflicting differences with an optimistic view towards life. Time passed, and life took another turn when I was in the Middle East. I was dramatically saved when sitting on board an aircraft which caught fire at 37,000 feet, and almost immediately, heard the call of God to preach and teach! Perhaps more of that later, that is my conversion story.

Eventually, this led to Bible College in Derbyshire and Theological College in London, and to pastoral ministry in Baptist churches, including a BMC in the city of London. By preaching across different networks and attending many evangelical and charismatic conferences, I gained a wider grasp of the Church of God in the UK. In addition to my call to pastoral ministry, I also responded to the call of God to become a secondary school teacher and managed, by the grace and the generosity of God, to intermingle both. In general terms, the twofold calling complemented each other.

Moving on from the personal glimpses and the influence of churches, my spiritual journey is just as complex. Biblically and theologically, my evangelical understanding of the Scriptures is rock solid, but I have avoided giving myself a classification much to the annoyance of some of my friends. Over the years there have been many movements or streams of spiritual renewal that have passed through heart and mind. Certainly, I have come to realise that I am forever learning to keep in step with the Spirit, and have often stumbled to read the signs of the times. Clearly, we are going through a period of transition in Britain at the present time, including cultural, racial, social, ethical and national changes by leaving the EU. Given that, I delight in all that God is doing across our four nations, but have concluded that there must be major radical changes across all networks if we are going to save the people from paganism and any of the other 'isms' that are emerging in the 21st century. What that means will be for others to decipher, but with less than 6% of the population (taken at Easter), attending church we would do well to reflect deeply what that is saying to us.

What we are facing in the UK is not just the decline of the church, but the abandonment of the Christian gospel. The churches, of whatever shape individually and corporately, will have to come on bended knee before God for a stay of execution for we are in a really desperate position. Many churches and leaders have feasted at the table of charismatic blessings, enjoyed the scene, and then abandoned the real guts of what it meant to be a really effective movement for God in line with the Early Church in the New Testament. Most churches, where there is evidence of life, still seem to be happy with the gentle rhythm of life that does not change the worshippers, let alone attempt to turn the world upside down. As I said, something has to change and hopefully there will be those who will be prepared to stand still, seek God, and see the salvation of gospel and church. If we are called to an everlasting preoccupation with God, and we are, we would do well to heed the words of A.W. Tozer:

> 'The world is perishing for lack of the knowledge of God and the Church is famishing for want of his presence' (The Pursuit of God, 1948, p 71). What he said then, applies equally to our time.

Preface

To attempt to write a book about spiritual engagement is no easy feat, but then this study is simply an overview of several themes. Factually, 'renewal movements' have perpetuated across the UK for over three hundred years. Without going through a long list, it is worth mentioning those that appeared to have made the biggest impact on the United Kingdom. The 17th century revivals under John Wesley and George Whitfield, the 1859 Revival across all the four nations, the 1904/5 Revival in the Welsh valleys, and the Sunderland, Lowestoft and Lewis local revivals (1920's-1950's). There have been other 'refreshing times' with the emergence of the Charismatic Movement, and the 'Toronto Blessing.' By and large these have long since gone in terms of their impact on churches, but it is vital that we never forget the positive features of those movements of God across the UK and other nations. Yes, there were mistakes and some damage may have been done, but when the Lord gives 'times of refreshing' with a view to strengthening and equipping the church, it would be churlish to rubbish what God has achieved through those experiences.

My concern is to give attention to the 'beginning of things' in terms of how we advance spiritually and practically. It has often puzzled me that while there has been much attention given to advancing the cause of Christ through the words of Jesus, there was less attention on the works of Jesus. Even at the best of times, it has to be acknowledged that large tracts of church life, be they charismatic or otherwise, have continually stalled due to the mysterious illness of insipid growth. In some respects, gospel people appear to be their own worst enemy by flitting from one 'new' way of doing the stuff, to doing virtually nothing to impact communities beyond the church door. Now, of course, there has been success in some areas, for example the BMC churches in London and Birmingham, and the sudden arrival of some thirty churches across the Midlands, running into the thousands of members each that did not exist thirty-five years ago. While acknowledging that, and other encouraging pockets of growth, there are still many areas across the nation where the 'fields may be white to harvest' but the Christian labourers are not just few, they are almost non-existent. Christian statisticians are brilliant at presenting a picture of the church of God across nations, which make fascinating and troubling reading, but that does little to address the issue of 'failed' growth. Perhaps, now is the time to return to basics – the basics of the Early Church – and begin again with the 'core values' and 'beliefs' of the pioneering apostolic bands. The themes chosen are in keeping with the aim of encouraging reflection that will drive us to abandon our stalemates, and move forward in faith towards the opportunities the Spirit of God will initiate within us and for us.

Inevitably, within those main themes there will be targeted areas that are part and parcel of the life of the Early Church. Reviewing the Gospels, the book of Acts, and some writings in the Epistles should wet our appetite to persevere not only over familiar areas, but be willing to start afresh. For example, whatever mediums we use today – and there is a constant flow emerging for our use – we need to be clear about our message and our methods.

Faith, spiritual authority and prophetic insights are a must when it comes to pursuing dynamic changes. And yes, there have been a number of recent activities through the establishment of hubs, the evangelistic 'Turning' outreach in Reading, and a variety of 'renewal movements' that offer the latest in Christian development. But fundamentally, there is a deeper need than simply following all the current 'moves' however good they appear, when really we need to return to the beginning and pursue 'core' elements that were part of the 1st Church. I can hear the cries, not again… but then every time the church of God does just that, and church history confirms that – there is transformation, growth and glory to God. And who, in any church community today, would not want that? The issue is one of reaching the point when we just stop what we are doing, stand back and look afresh at the New Testament and with prophetic insight, start afresh. Can that be done? Yes, it can. Are leaders prepared to do that? Well, how we respond to an opportunity to do it again is based on dynamic prayer, a fresh anointing of the Spirit, a prophetic perspective and hearts filled with the fire of God. There is every possibility of seeing Jesus Christ crucified, risen, exalted and glorified to the praise of our God and Heavenly Father in the present decade can we not therefore say? Even so, 'Come Lord Jesus' (Rev. 22: 20).

A Perspective

The sovereign purpose of God has always been to build the kingdom of the gospel of Jesus Christ and populate the planet with a new humanity – the Church of God. The plan of this book is to draw attention to what is possible with those same people, under the calling and authority of Christ. However we define 'the faith once delivered to the saints' we do live in a very challenging and unforgiving age, but the Lord has not left himself without witnesses. Worldwide, the Church of God is still the most powerful society on planet earth, with resources in God that is way beyond the machinations of Satanic darkness that resist and attempt to destroy what God has purposed for the present and the future. That is where, *Breaking-through and Reaching-out* is an attempt to refocus our eyes on Jesus, and capture what he has planned by charging the believing community into walking afresh in faith and supernatural ministry to fulfil the calling of God. The areas of study are familiar so there is nothing essentially new, but reviewing the familiar will help us to recover what many leaders and churches have lost, which is vital for progression into a necessary new dedication to the truths that are everlastingly vital for God's honour and glory (Heb. 12: 22-28). In that regard, under the same central theme, there are two volumes. Book 1 is subtitled: A Call to Engage – Enjoying the Presence – Today, which centres on the dynamics of the Kingdom of God. I have followed John Bright's view that the theme of the kingdom of God is one of the great unifying concepts close to the total message of the Bible (The Kingdom of God in Bible and Church, 1955). To call believers back to a concept that many of us have been engaged with for some years is no mean challenge. Some readers might argue that they have frequently listened to and heard teaching on the topic. Be that as it may, it is my observation that many churches, of various theological persuasions, may be familiar with the concept but rarely is that played out in the nitty-gritty of regular activities in church life. In fact, I can guarantee that little or nothing is taught on this subject from one year to the next, thereby limiting believers from enjoying a kingdom lifestyle. Jesus was the one person, after John the Baptist, who dropped a theological bomb among the people when he announced that the 'kingdom of God is among you' – the new age had arrived! To test this lack of understanding I suggest that church leaders ask people to tell them what they understand about the kingdom of God. I believe the response by many will be blank stares. It is just not very high on their spiritual agenda. Thus the importance of bringing this great theme to the attention of believers, hoping they might see the value of this thrilling topic. The idea of 'kingdom' runs through the entire text in the Old and New Testaments. To highlight this vital truth with the following adjoining biblical truths should enrich us all as we examine what the Spirit wants to teach us. The connected themes in Book 1 draw our attention to the ministry of Jesus, the work of the Spirit, the importance of belonging, believing and behaving. The demanding nature of the Gospel of the good news brings about transformation – from the beginning of the Christian life to a way of life that is part of celebrating constant on-going change which leads to growth and development. Living and dying in the Spirit is far from easy, yet such is the nature of discipleship that communities emerge to bring about a 'new order' for humanity – a new age – God's age, through Christ. For all believers, it is really time to get on board and enjoy the ride.

Book 2, carries on under the same banner 'Breaking Through and Reaching Out', but like Book 1 demands that we come face to face with another call - A Call to Ignite – because living in the Spirit concentrates the Christian on God's on-going work in the life of the believer and church. We will give attention to the 'intoxicating experience of God's action in our lives' for the benefit of all – both believer and nonbeliever. It is an astonishing fact that beyond the doors of the church – people do live – but they live with constant agendas and addictions that do them no good. The church, sadly seems to be deaf to the many 'plagues' that batter so many people. No, this is not about Covid, though it does seem to do damage to too many people. We don't disregard that modern phenomenon, but seek to see the value of offering something that brings about dynamic alteration to personal living. The way forward is to hear and listen to the 'gospel songs' – the songs of life – songs of triumph – songs that tell the old biblical story. God has not gone away, so it behoves us to march in step with his step if we are going to see radical change in our society that appears to become more and more corrupt as the days go by. My advice to every believer is to 'hear what the Spirit is saying to the churches' and to the world at large – and that we aim to apply truth in Book 2 to lifestyles and congregations – we hope you find time to read both books.

One of the significant passages of teaching in the New Testament is about the value of authority – spiritual authority is to be found in Paul's Letter to the Church in Ephesus: Eph 1: 17-22:

"I do not cease to give thanks for you, remembering you in my prayers, that the God of our Lord Jess Christ, the Father of glory, may give you the Spirit of wisdom and of revelation in the knowledge of him, having the eyes of your hearts enlightened that you may know what is the hope to which he has called you, what are the riches of his glorious inheritance in the saints, and what is the immeasurable greatness of his power toward us who believe, according to the working of his great might that he worked in Christ when he raised him from the dead and seated him at his right hand in the heavenly places, far from above all rule and authority and power and dominion, and above every name that is named, not only in this age but also in the one to come. And he put all things under his feet and gave him as head over all things to the church, which is his body, the fullness of him who fills all in all" (ESV).

PART 1
Releasing the Kingdom - Today

Mark Driscoll, an American Pastor, has argued like many of us in the UK that Christendom is dead in western nations. Mark was responsible for planting Mars Hill Church in Seattle in 1996. He writes:

> "With the help of a small group of broke, newly converted, single rockers trying to reach a city that had more dogs and cats than children and evangelical Christians. He admitted that there were times when things went wrong, and they failed, which should have slowed down the growth of the gospel. Thankfully, it didn't for they started with a motley crew of arty people in a living room of a rental home, with literally nothing but an open Bible and open hearts. Out of that insignificant start a church was built one changed life at a time. It became one of the nation's largest and fastest-growing churches in the United States, based upon an hour plus of Bible preaching every week. It made no sense. Every time the media asked what the secret is, we tell them the same thing: it does not matter who is against you if Jesus is with you. Many of the new believers are young, single, college educated, not virgins, who have spent more time with porn than with Paul. They represent the first generation of their families, breaking decades of unbelief, perversion, addiction and folly" (M. Driscoll, A Call to Resurgence, Tyndale, 2013, 3-5).

Unfortunately, addiction is at an all-time high in our nation across many generations, from teens to people in their sixties plus. For the last thirty years or so, there has been a movement across many people groups where, sexual perversion is no longer teenagers making hay while the sun shines. Sexual experimentation is as prominent among the older generations as it is among the 20s-40s. Porn is almost a constant feature at parties and events, as is drug-taking – even at what would have been classed as a 'safe' get together. Girls and women are targeted constantly to show off their bodies while taking payments for the same. Increasingly, there appears to be little shame as people stumble around for the next fix – be it drugs or sex or some complicated perversion, hoping for some kind of high. Culturally, it is now apparent that fraud, cheating, stealing, robbing ordinary people, has become par for the course by some insurance companies and banks. Huge bonuses are grabbed by the CEO's or directors of companies who are handed huge sums of money annually. The social mores are being trampled left right and centre for the justice system is broken, and people are left high and dry without any chance of returns of money stolen. The nation is constantly swallowing addiction after addiction such is the low level of moral purity. So, there it is, the same issues again – money, sex and power. So, where is the church in all this? Well, for the most part it seems to carry on without realising what is happening around it. Yes, it dives into some areas by helping the poor, the neglected and the disenfranchised. Sadly, its attempts at racial harmony has only been superficial, and there is a growing demand for the community of God's people to be more active in this area. Let us hope and pray that the days ahead will see the church marching again with banners flying, as it proclaims the gospel of the kingdom of God into those areas of moral depravity.

Reflection

Magic Kingdom or Jesus' Kingdom?

When Patricia Gearing buried her daughter in a cemetery near Mablethorpe, Lincolnshire, in 1998, she placed a simple cross on her grave. The local council officials told her to remove it, since 'crosses are discouraged.' In its place she asked permission to erect a headstone featuring Mickey Mouse and was told that the authorities were happy with that! The magic kingdom of Disney exercises a persuasive influence in our society. Its symbols even have the power to displace the traditional symbols of the Christian faith. The kingdom of Disney purveys a set of values based on the mainstream American dream, based on a nostalgic past while pointing customers to an optimistic future. Disney's romantic interpretations of the past and optimistic predictions of the future are designed to make people escape the present. But once the visit has been made, the film watched or the merchandise purchased, today's reality has an ugly habit of reasserting itself. The magic wears off. The truth is that nothing has changed.

How different is the kingdom of Jesus. The kingdom of Jesus transforms and embraces reality. Jesus not only encountered evil but overcame it by embracing it on the cross (Col. 2: 15). Tom Smail puts it well:

> 'Christ comes to the cross as the fireman comes to the fire, as the lifeboat comes to the sinking ship, as the rescue team comes to the wounded man in the alpine snow. They have what it takes to help and deliver.' (Sermon, June, 1979, Portsmouth).

So Christ on the cross comes to where the Father, in his holy wrath has handed over sinners to the consequences of their sin. In stepping into the void, Jesus' redemptive action, brought 'peace through his blood, shed on the cross'(Col. 1: 20). This is reality and not fantasy and make-believe. Jesus' kingdom is the REAL kingdom.

The Bible opens with the statement, "In the beginning God ..." (Gen. 1: 1). Just that – God is. There is no attempt to prove the existence of God. This truth that 'God is' is stated throughout Scripture. And in reading through the bible it soon becomes obvious that God is not only omnipotent, omniscience, omnipresent but sovereign. The sovereign or kingdom acts of God are ways of understanding who God is, and how God behaves. No matter whether you are in the Old or New Testament, the story is a story of a God who acts constantly and surprisingly, in keeping with his character, and providentially directs all things (Ps. 103: 19; Rom. 11: 36; 1 Cor. 15: 27; Eph. 1: 11). The way to identify this surprise is to see God's presence and purpose, enshrined in the kingdom of God teaching and life that is part and parcel of both testaments. Throughout God is King – King over everything in heaven and earth. Clearly, the 'rule' of God is to be found throughout the bible from Genesis to Revelation. John Bright, the Old Testament scholar, comments:

> "The concept of the kingdom of God involves, in a real sense, the total message of the bible... To grasp what is meant by the kingdom of God, is to come very close to the heart of the bible's gospel of salvation" (The Kingdom of God in Bible and Church, 1955, 7).

Overall the word 'kingdom' appears over two hundred times in the Old Testament, using 5 Hebrew words, whereas in the New Testament the word is used nearly one hundred and fifty times. The kingdom of God (Gk: basileia tou Theou) and the kingdom of heaven (Gk: basileia tou ouranon) are interchangeable and appear one hundred and nineteen times in the Gospels. In the meantime, Christians of every generation are called to be actively engaged in pursuing what God had intended right from the beginning of time - the establishment of a kingdom which will form the basis of the final kingdom community in that far off day, at the end of time.

Believing is Seeing

Seeing the truths of God's sovereign actions as biblically recorded provides us with a global perspective of his total plan for humankind. The five rings, an adaption from another source, allow us to see common links between each 'ringed theme' and thereby provides a bigger vision of God's intentions. The only authentic story of God we have is found in the pages of the Scriptures (Old and New Testaments).

These narratives not only share the essential nature and attributes of God, but also provide insights into God's transcendence and immanence. The kingdom element is prominent in the narratives of both Testaments and is a constant theme throughout the sixty six books of the bible. The word 'kingdom' is scarce in certain recorded events, but does not mean that it is not present in other forms. Take the Psalms for instance, where the word rarely appears, yet every song seems to confirm that God is very much in charge of the cosmos. It is also worth recognising that the Psalter was written over many decades, and always pictures the overarching benefits to God's people if they remain faithful. That feature undergirds the way God's sovereign actions are brought together. The story of God's being and actions are pursued through these five interlocking ringed stories:

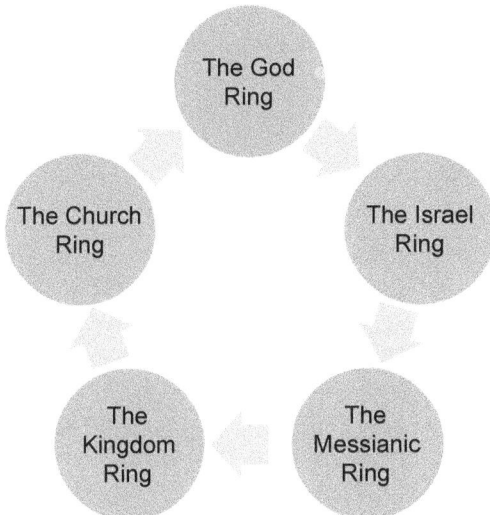

The God Ring

These stories are connected in the writings of both Testaments. Take the apostle Paul: "Therefore I glory in Christ Jesus in my service to God (and) I will not ... speak of anything except what Christ has accomplished through me in leading the Gentiles to obey God by what I have said and done" (Rom. 15; 17-18). Through the story of Israel and the story of Jesus, the Gentile world has been offered the blessings of the covenant of Abraham (Gen. 12: 2; Gal. 3: 8). As a result of the mercy and grace of God both Jew and Gentile come together to be one 'new people – the Church' (Eph. 2: 13, 19). The five rings give us an insight into God's glorious plan, through the provision of salvation for human kind, through the atoning death of Jesus Christ on the cross, and his physical resurrection from the grave (Acts 15: 3-8; 1 Pet. 3: 18).

To open the pages of the Bible is to be confronted with a God who is, for his existence is never explained. In a sense, God is taken for granted in that his existence is just stated, but he exists not only for himself but also for the world of humanity. In fact, whenever God is mentioned in the Scriptures the words: grace, mercy, justice, love and glory are never far away. God is unique as Father, Son and Holy Spirit – the Tri-unity who, as sovereign Lord overseas everything in heaven and earth. Therefore, according to the texts, in the Old and New Testament, each member is co-divine, co-equal and co-eternal with one another, for their unity is sacrosanct. Yet, God is not some impersonal power, but a **personal God** who is Spirit, who transcends the entire world order and deserves to be worshipped:

> 'To reflect upon God in his three-in-oneness, Father, Son, Spirit, in their distinguishable persons and functions yet perfect unity and harmony in mutual, everlasting love, is to catch a vision of something so unspeakably glorious, even beautiful ... that it has ... moved men and women to heights of adoring worship, love and praise: Holy, holy, holy, merciful and mighty, God in three persons, Blessed Trinity!' (B. Milne Know the Truth IVP p 63).

The Israel Ring

The story of God's pilgrim people is set out in the Old Testament. In being the 'chosen-ones' Israel represented God to other peoples (Dt. 7: 7-12). This loving choice was based on God's sovereign decision as his divine right. From the call of Abraham and the embryonic beginnings of a people through Isaac, the formation of Israel was grounded in the purposes of God (Gen. 12: 1; 21: 1-3). The actions of God, through Moses, resulted in an exhibition of 'signs and wonders' leading to Israel fleeing from the 'house of bondage' (Egypt) towards the land promised by the Lord. The Passover event by which they won their freedom, confirmed by their Red Sea baptism, became the focal point of their on-going history (Ex. 6: 6; 7: 3; 12: 12, 40; 14: 26-28 Ps. 78). The Torah describes their 'wilderness wanderings' until they enter the Promised Land (Josh. 3: 1-5). Their continued history through the prophets, priests and kings created a nation-state. Israel became established and for several centuries maintained their special relationship with God (Heb. Yahweh). Eventually, due to constant disobedience they lost their way, their vision, and their land as they faced first one exile (Israel) in 721 BC, and then a second exile (Judah) in 586 BC. God maintained his affection for them because of his covenant with them and out of the Babylonian exile, a remnant of Israel emerged (Mal. 3: 17). As their history moved towards a new era, their promised Messiah-Jesus appeared, born of a virgin named Mary, who would in time save the people from their sins (Mt. 1: 18-25).

The Messiah-Christ Ring

For hundreds of years Christians have insisted that Messiah-Christ is present in the Old Testament as well as in the New Testament. From the opening chapters of the bible there are clear references to this central figure (Gen. 3: 15; 14: 18). Frequently, King David and the prophet Isaiah spoke of the coming 'King of kings and Lord of lords' as they viewed God's plan and purpose (Ps. 16: 8-1; 110: 1; Isa. 7: 14; 9: 6-7; 53: 1-12; 61: 1-3). A central truth about Yeshua (Jesus) was the prediction of a 'suffering servant' who, as Messiah, would die gloriously on a Roman cross. That one voluntary act of God for all humankind resulted in the offer of salvation (2 Pet. 3: 9). Such an action resulted in the defeat of sin, disease, death and Satan (Eph. 2: 1-6; 1 Jn. 3: 8). Through his death, resurrection, ascension and exaltation, Christ entered glory having completed his work on earth. He continued his ministry from his throne in heaven, by interceding for the saints on earth. From heaven, He baptised the people with the Holy Spirit on the Feast of Pentecost, while awaiting his eventual return at the end of the Age (Eph. 1: 18-22; Acts 2: 4; Phil. 2: 6-11).

The Kingdom Ring

In the Bible the word 'kingdom' means 'authority with the rule of a king.' The Psalmist sang, "his kingdom rules overall" (Ps. 103: 19). It is God who gives and establishes the kingdom (1 Chron. 29: 11). To read the books of the Old Testament is to be confronted with a God that is not only sovereign, but displays that sovereignty over people, tribes, communities and nations. His 'rule' is seen in the first and last page of the old dispensation (Gen. 1: 1 Mal. 4: 1-6). For centuries the people had been waiting for the kingdom to come – for the Messiah to appear. Isaiah the prophet, put it into song:

> "How beautiful upon the mountains are the feet of him who brings good news ...who proclaim salvation, who says to Zion, 'Your God reigns!' (Isa. 52: 7). Therefore, "Arise, shine; for your light has come, and the glory of the Lord has risen upon you ..." (Isa. 60: 1ff.)

Such predictions of the coming glorious reign of God, gave hope to the people so that when John the Baptist proclaimed: "Repent, for the kingdom of heaven is at hand" (Mt. 3: 2-3). There was heightened excitement in Judah for the King to come. When Jesus preached the reign of God, breaking Satan's control over suffering, sin, disease and death, there was an atmosphere of peace, joy, freedom and thanksgiving. The Messianic prophecies were at last being fulfilled (Isa. 35: 6). No wonder people glorified God when they saw the miraculous signs and wonders being used to bring release to the captives (Lk. 4: 18). To be part of this kingdom is to be born from above by the Holy Spirit, for there is no other way of entry (Jn. 3: 3, 7). The kingdom then, now and in the future, is about the eschatological reign of God for 'it has come' (Mt. 28: 18). This kingdom can become fully manifest only when Jesus Christ returns to earth (Eph. 1: 9-10; Rev. 1: 5-7).

The Church Ring

The Gospels open with a declaration about the kingdom of God by Jesus, "The kingdom of God is near. Repent and believe the gospel" (Mk. 1: 15). Later in his ministry, due to the revelation to Peter that Jesus was the Messiah, he announced:

> "I will build my church, and the gates of hell shall not prevail against it" (Mt. 16: 18).

The purpose of the coming of the Son of God was to establish a company of people – a kingdom community that would last forever. Such a community, which began in the Gospels and Pentecost (Acts 2: 38-39, 41), has been described as a family, a flock, a vineyard, a body, a bride, a building and an army (Eph. 2: 9; 1 Pet. 5: 1-3; Jn. 15: 1-5; 1 Cor. 12: 12; 1 Cor. 3: 9; Eph. 5: 22-33; Eph. 6: 10-12). Christians, those born of the Spirit (Jn. 3: 3), are also born into the family of God – the church (1 Cor. 12: 12). In the New Testament, the church is always people, not a building and is founded "on the apostles and prophets, with Christ Jesus as the chief cornerstone" (Eph. 2: 20). Two Greek words are used to define the church: 'kyriakos' (Greek) which means 'the house of the Lord' and 'ekklesia' (Greek) meaning 'assembly.' The church celebrates its togetherness for "There is neither Jew nor Greek, slave nor free male nor female, for you are all one in Christ Jesus" (Gal. 3: 28), thereby enjoying multiracial, multicultural and multi-generational people groups. The church was born of the Spirit on Pentecost and it is impossible to have church without the Spirit (Acts 2: 4). There is no life in the church without the Spirit, for he empowers the church in worship, witness, ministry, prayer, guidance, confirms truth, promotes mission and unites in love (John. 4: 24; Acts 1: 8; 1 Cor. 12: 4-11; Rom. 8: 28; 8: 14; John. 16: 13; Luke. 24: 49; Eph. 4: 25-32).

Kingdom Consciousness

The five rings overview provide insight into God's determination into transforming planet Earth and its peoples. God is so self-authenticating that he does not need humankind to deliver his objective, but has chosen to work with us to complete his purpose for his glory and our benefit. This 'Gospel of God' is nothing less than a supernatural message in word and action, that change becomes almost endemic. Yes, there is faith – faith that believes –and we are invited to join in with him to proclaim and demonstrate that same gospel – the gospel of the kingdom of God. True though that is, the call now is for the present church of the living God to **release the kingdom today**. This means that believers are called upon in our time, to pursue and demonstrate the gospel of Jesus, like the disciples and the early church. Alongside 'building a kingdom community' in and through the Church of God, we have been chosen to follow the teaching of Christ and model the acts of supernatural ministry. For too long we have talked about the truth of the kingdom, now is the time when, under God, individual believers and churches, as led by Spirit are invited to follow the early Christians and demonstrate kingdom truths: 'preach this message: The kingdom of heaven is near.' Heal the sick, raise the dead, cleanse those who have leprosy, drive out demons. Freely you have received, freely give" (Matt. 10: 7-8). In a word, release the kingdom message – today!

Reflection

A group of believers were in a prayer room in a church building, when there was a commotion by the open door of the Baptist church. They went to investigate, only to find a man (the father) struggling with a teenage boy (the son), pulling him into the building. He shouted to the elderly believers that his son, when passing a cross on a church would fly into a rage, have a convulsive fit and roll about on the floor. As they wondered what to do, the father pushed him into the room where the Christians had been praying. He immediately fitted, fell to the floor, the believers began praying 'in the name of Jesus.' Prior to this, the prayer team had been reading from the Gospel of Luke about a possessed boy being healed by Jesus (Lk. 9: 39-43). So they prayed, and began to see God working, for the lad was restored, sat up and chatted with his older 'new friends'. This was certainly a 'God moment' for within weeks Michael openly confessed Christ, was baptized, received the Spirit and became active within the church and community (Acts 2: 38; Rom. 10: 9-10). It turned out that he had had convulsive fits for years; underwent medical examinations by doctors, including a psychiatrist. They failed to find the reason behind the fits. The day he fitted in the prayer room was after he had seen the cross on the front of the church building. His reaction to the cross was a puzzle, but the medics had concluded that he may have had some kind of religious encounter which he would grow out of! The Christian's who were involved in this 'faith' moment rarely talked about it. For them, the Gospel stories were factual narratives of the way King Jesus extended his kingdom by saving and healing people both then and now. Thankfully, there is a growing sense among church leaders and churches, that kingdom consciousness is a positive feature of the 21st century church in the UK.

Certainly, 'kingdom consciousness' is essential for believers for without that sense of the value of the kingdom dimension, the Scriptures will be deeply misunderstood. The kingdom is God's kingdom (Gk: basileia tou theou); for every aspect of the kingdom is derived from the character and action of God. The presence of the kingdom is to be understood from the nature of God's present activity; and the future is the manifestation of his kingly rule at the end of the age. Thereby linking a common overview of the life and ministry of Jesus, for Mark begins his Gospel with a declaration: "The beginning of the gospel of Jesus Christ, the Son of God" (Mk. 1: 1). In fact, all four Gospels provide us with a panoramic view and biography of the life, ministry, death and resurrection of Jesus. Matthew focuses on Jesus as King, Mark as the Son of Man, Luke as the Saviour of the world, and John as the Son of God. Each of these titles fits in with the Messianic figure outlined in the Old Testament. The word 'gospel' comes from the Greek word 'euangelion,' which is used in the New Testament to announce the 'good news.' This gospel would be heralded by apostles, prophets, evangelists, pastor-teachers and the 'Laos' members of churches who would declare the good news in cities, towns, communities and nations. Often the message of the good news, contained the message of love and forgiveness, but also included the need for repentance, alongside judgement as a means of correction and renewal. Each of the four Gospels presents a colourful variety of scenes about who Jesus was, and what he said and did. The New Testament writers, inspired by the Holy Spirit, act as witnesses as they retell the story of the Kingly Messiah.

The Teacher

According to the blurb given by teacher training institutions there are three kinds of teachers: There are those you can listen to; there are those you can't listen to; and there are those you want to listen to. Jesus was the third kind of teacher. Every Gospel writer has references to the marvellous teaching ability of Jesus. His disciples, the religious elders, Pharisees and scribes refer to him as a teacher – a rabbi (Mark 1: 21; 4: 38; Matt. 5: 2; Luke 4: 31; Matt. 21: 23; Luke 20: 21). In John, Nicodemus said, 'Rabbi, we know you are a teacher come from God. For no one could perform the miraculous signs you are doing if God were not with him' (3: 2). The teaching of Jesus had specific characteristics which are noted in the four Gospels. There are five aspects to his teaching:

Jesus taught with <u>authority</u>, an authority that came from the throne of heaven (Matt. 28: 18) and can be summed up in the words, 'For I did not speak on my own accord, but the Father who sent me commanded me what to say and how to say it. I know that his command leads to eternal life. So whatever I say is just what the Father has told me to say' (John 12: 49-50). No matter what Jesus said, whether a story, a parable, a declaration, a direction, 'the Sermon on the Mount,' he was speaking for his Father every time he spoke. The religious leaders were as dumfounded as the disciples and the crowds, for no other teacher taught like Jesus (Matt. 7: 29; 9: 6).

Jesus, acknowledged that his authoritative teaching was due to his '<u>anointing in the Spirit</u>' at his baptism in the Jordan by John the Baptist (Luke 3: 21-23). He confirmed the purpose of his 'baptism in the Spirit' when reading from Isaiah 61 in the synagogue at Nazareth: 'The Spirit of the Sovereign Lord is on me, because the Lord has anointed me to preach the good news to the poor. He has sent me to bind up the broken-hearted, to proclaim freedom for the captives and release from darkness for the prisoners, to proclaim the year of the Lord's favour … (61; 1-2; cf. Luke 4: 18-19). There was never a time when Jesus was without the presence of the Spirit, for he remained indefinitely upon him until the day he died (John 1: 33; 19: 30). Jesus had supernatural ability from the time of his baptism, and it was this that convinced his listeners that he was speaking God's own truth. On one occasion, when some of his disciples got cold feet because they found his teaching too strong, his response was to tell them that:

> "The Spirit gives life, the flesh counts for nothing. The words
> I have spoken to you are spirit and they are life" (John 6: 63).

Jesus' teaching was <u>revelatory</u> for he was speaking the 'words of God' and unveiling to the disciples, the people, and the authorities, that only his teaching was acceptable to heaven, and was the means of bringing about transformational change in people's lives. If the people listened to the 'truth' they will be 'set free' and 'if the Son sets' them free they 'will be free indeed' (John 8: 32, 36). Again, Jesus himself is 'the way and the truth and the life. No one comes to the Father except through me' (John 14: 6). The teaching of Jesus was based on his intimacy with his Father (Luke 5: 16). His key topic was the kingdom of God, which was both present and future, for it was 'among them' but still 'to come' (Luke 10: 9; Matt. 3: 2). It was all about revelation from God, through Jesus, to the people.

Jesus teaching was imaginative for much of it was <u>visual</u>, for his style aimed to capture the imagination of his hearers. He drew pictures with his stories, he gave clues to what God was like, 'Anyone who has seen me has seen the Father' (John 14: 9; 5: 17). So, by looking at him they have a picture of God, our heavenly Father! He then presented himself as the 'I am's of God' for I am 'the light of the world,' 'the bread of life,' 'the good shepherd,' and 'the true Vine' (John 8: 12; 6: 35; 10: 11; 15: 1). The phrase 'I am' would take the listeners back into the time of Moses (Exodus 3: 14) when the patriarch had the audacity to ask Yahweh, 'who are you' and back came the reply, 'I am that I am.' In a word, 'I am God' so as Jesus stands before them he is bearing witness that he is 'one with the Father' God himself in human form.

Jesus teaching was <u>compassionately relevant</u> to the disciples and the people for he regarded them as 'harassed and helpless, like sheep without a shepherd' (Matt. 9: 36). The crowds that followed him from Judea, Samaria, Galilee and Decapolis were caught up in pursuing the greatest teacher the world has ever heard or seen. The Synoptic Gospels give the impression that, in the first two years of Jesus ministry, they followed him in their thousands. The feeding of the 5,000 and the 4,000 showed they just could not get enough of him both for his teaching and for the miracles they witnessed (Matt. 14: 13-21; 15: 29-38). The spirit of compassion flooded Jesus' heart so often that people were often healed just by being in or near the crowd (Mark 1: 21-2: 12). When teaching the Sermon on the Mount, Jesus did so, not just for the disciples, but also for the crowds, as he talked about a new way of living in God's kingdom (Matt. 5: 1-7: 29).

Learning is vital for kingdom people

To have had a double calling to be both a pastor-teacher and a secondary school pastoral manager, has given me many opportunities to try and understand the way people learn, whether they are adults or 11-18 years of age. Timetables for teaching staff mean, depending on your role within the school, that in one day a teacher could be facing five different age groups or learning groups. This means that for that day the teacher could have two academic lessons (GCSE and 'A' level), and three lower school lessons (7, 8, 9). Each class demands from the teacher a different way of teaching, and if your teaching approach is interactive, the demands on the teacher to produce the right attitude, style, information and learning plan is an immense challenge. At the end of the day the teacher has to review what has been taught, how it has been taught and find out exactly what the pupils have learned in those lessons. Such a day, and such a demand, is not unusual but it costs in term of time, energy, observation and hopefully your conclusion could be that lessons seemed to go well. In the pastorate, there may be one or two services, Sunday morning and evening, and if you are teaching you are ministering God's truth from the Scriptures to adults, teenagers and children. In the modern world you may not see the people at the service until the following week, so the questions are still the same as the teachers, did you handle message well, what did the people hear and what did they learn and was God glorified?

At this juncture let's consider the following table as a means of trying to understand what happened in both spheres for learning is a huge challenge because:

>We learn only 10% of what we hear

>We learn only 15% of what we see

>We learn only 20% of what we hear and see

>We learn only 40% of what we discuss with others

>We learn 80% of what we experience directly.

Also, there are three principled ways of learning for teachers:

> There is the <u>Visual</u> way of learning for 29% of us prefer learning by seeing.
>
> There is the <u>Auditory</u> way of learning for 34% of us enjoy communicating with and learning by sound including the spoken word.
>
> There is the <u>Kinaesthetic</u> way of learning for 29% of us prefer to engage in the physical experience.

We do, to some extent, utilise all three principles. But just as we each have a hand preference, an ear preference, an eye preference and a brain hemisphere preference, we also have a representational system preference. It's a funny old world – learning!

What is obvious, from the perspective of pastoral teaching/preaching, is that the Scriptures are distinct from any other writing, and combined with the work of the Holy Spirit, the hearers can and will be deeply affected if they are open to what God has been saying. This is reinforced by the writer of Hebrews: 'For the word of God is living and active, sharper than any two edged sword, it penetrates even to dividing soul and spirit, joints and marrow; it judges the thoughts and attitudes of the heart' (4: 12) Furthermore, 'when he, the Spirit of truth comes, he will guide you into all truth. He will not speak on his own, he will speak only what he hears, and he will tell you what is yet to come. He will bring glory to me' (John 16: 13-14). Preachers and teachers will confirm that Jesus used all three ways to share the message of the kingdom of God.

> J. John puts it succinctly when he notes:
>
> It's not what they say, it's what they hear
>
> It's not just what they hear, It's what they see
>
> It's not just the message, It's the meaning
>
> It's not just the truth, but the relevance of what we say
>
> It's not what people like about our sermons that matters, but what they do

(Preach the Word, J. John, SW 2006, 13).

In his Gospel Mark included an announcements by Jesus, setting out the kind of ministry he would be engaged in, "The time is fulfilled, and kingdom of God is at hand;   Repent and believe the gospel" (Mk. 1: 15 ESV).   What then does Jesus mean when he refers to the kingdom of God?   The word itself can refer to a realm, a domain, a principality or a rule – the rule of God.   To speak of the kingdom is to recall that God is the sovereign Lord, for "the earth is the Lord's and the fullness therefore, the world and those who dwell therein …" Ps. 24: 1).   We may say that 'God rules' and the world is in subjugation to him and under God's oversight, but at present we do not see everything subject to him" (Heb. 2 8).   The complete rule of God will come in the future when, "the kingdom of the world has become the kingdom of our Lord Jesus Christ" (Rev. 11 15).   In the meantime, Jesus preached that the kingdom had actually appeared in his very person.   In a word, the kingdom of God was his sovereign way of dealing with humankind.   It was in the synagogue in Nazareth, Jesus' home town that he set out the dynamic nature of his mission:

> "God's Spirit is on me; he's chosen me to preach the Message of good news to the poor, Sent me to announce pardon … recovery of sight … To set the burdened and battered free, to announce, 'This is God's year to act!" (Luke 4 18-19, The Message).

Prior to his public announcement in Nazareth, Jesus was baptized in the river Jordon by his cousin, John the Baptist. His baptism was cataclysmic, in that the heavens opened, God spoke and Jesus was anointed by the Spirit to empower him to minister to a broken and needy world. Obviously, Jesus' ministry was centred on the kingdom of God, which is mentioned over eighty times in the Gospels.   This topic was not new to the Jewish community because it appeared regularly in the Old Testament, especially in the prophetic books.   They were, at the time of Jesus, conscious of the idea behind God's coming Messiah and kingdom, but had a jaundiced view as to what was meant by both.   In their eyes the Messiah would be an all-powerful king, not unlike David who would have a physical kingdom, lead the 'new Israel' to defeat the

Romans and free the land from the contamination of the goyem (Heb: the Gentiles). Their views contradicted what was taught in the Tenack (the Hebrew Old Testament) which described a spiritual kingdom and not a physical kingdom. Jesus corrected the false teaching the people had learned in the synagogues and by the temple teachers. He provided two ways to understand God's kingdom through his teaching sermons and parables, and by proclamation and demonstration of the truths of God put into practice.

The Kingdom of God

The synoptic Gospels, (Matthew, Mark, and Luke) all contain Jesus' teaching on the kingdom of God. Each of the Gospel writers, witnessed most of the events in the life and ministry of Jesus, and collected and collated what they heard and saw. At some point their notes or parchments were painstakingly put together and the Gospels emerged. Obviously, with three authors writing about the Nazarene, there was bound to be overlap and sharing of some texts, but that simply makes the documents more authentic. In coming to the teachings of Jesus, we are confronted with the greatest teacher who ever lived, and the greatest teaching that has ever been given. Yet, teaching and preaching can have its problems!

> **Reflection**
>
> Theological institutions for Baptist trainees for church leadership face two 'sermon classes' (experiences during their 3 or 4 years at Theological College). The class is held in the chapel in front of the faculty and the whole student body, so it can be full of tension, anxiety or even hope! The student is encouraged to preach a 'normal' sermon of about 20 minutes on a theme or passage of Scripture he or she is familiar with. It is common after such a sermon that the student faces two critics from among the students, and comments by two of the faculty. Staff and students leave the chapel and remove to the college common room for the deliberations. On one occasion, one of the older students – and ex-navy officer – was to preach

before this august body. He did so, managing to keep to the time, but on his journey through the Bible most were having difficulty following the sermon. Whether it was the constant references to 'navy jargon' or some other mysterious 'tick,' we became entangled in his talk. Anyway, the first critic, a student from his own year admitted he knew nothing about the navy, but said he was certain of one thing, 'no navy ship fires off all its guns at the same time'! The image brought the house down, with lots of laughter – not at the preacher – but just at the idea of a sermon, blasting off in all directions. Thankfully, he was rescued by the faculty members and was assured that he had a future in the pulpit, but to avoid using too many navy metaphors (The 'sermon class' approach has now been modified).

The Sermons

The 'sermons' given by Jesus had an authority that impacted all who heard him teach. His Spirit-anointed teaching presented truths that connected with the past history of Israel, and took the listeners into a world they had never come across before. True, the Rabbi's taught the Old Testament, gave parable stories, used nature to describe God's truths, but not one taught that God's kingdom was for all the people – Jew, Gentile and even Samaritans. All his sermons were kingdom based.

> He taught the 'Sermon on the Mount' (Matthew) and/or the 'Sermon on the Plain' (Luke). The teaching themes in the sermon were very significant for the disciples. He covered a wide range of topics, the essence of which is to live by being and doing, providing a 'new law' for a new age. The principles and practices Jesus presented were radical, revolutionary and transformative. To the question, 'Who is the Sermon for' three views have emerged:The Sermon is for everyone. The Sermon explains how to become a disciple. The Sermon is about being a disciple.

If this is a 'discipleship document' and it is clear that it is, the teaching is for those who are followers of Jesus Christ. To create a new humanity a foundational message was crucial for all believers, for this message framed the background to the supernatural. The teaching is thought-provoking and demanding, but Jesus was calling people to commit to a different kind of lifestyle, saying: 'live like this and enjoy the kingdom of heaven.' The Sermon may be divided into three parts:

Section 1 – Righteousness (5: 1-48)

Discipleship was one of the ways in which Jesus would begin to build his kingdom community and, with the crowd in the background, Jesus set out the principles for the people of God. The characteristics of the followers are to be 'blessed' (Gk: makarios, happy), if they are poor in spirit, mourn, are meek, hunger for righteousness, are merciful, pure in heart, become peacemakers, rejoice when persecuted (Matt. 5: 1-12). They are to be salt and light, keep God's law, avoid murder, adultery, divorce and avoid oath-making, no tit for tat, turn the other cheek, and love their enemies (Matt. 5: 13-48).

Section 2 - Reformation (6: 1-34)

Acts of righteousness are to be done without grandstanding, and include giving, praying, fasting, storing treasure in heaven, serving one master, and avoiding anxiety (Matt. 6: 1-34). The prayer dimension was a crucial aspect of being 'right with God,' so they are to pray:

> "Our Father in heaven hallowed be your name, your kingdom come, your will be done on earth as it is in heaven. Give us today our daily bread. Forgive us our trespasses. And lead us not into temptation, but deliver us from evil, for yours is the kingdom and the power and the glory forever. Amen" (6: 9-13)

Jesus calls disciples to, 'seek first the kingdom of God and his righteousness, and all these things will be given to you (ordinary things) as well' (6: 33).

Section 3 – Relationship (7: 1-29)

Judging, a common attitude, has to be forfeited if used wrongly, but asking, seeking and knocking will bring riches from God, but they are to avoid wide gates and choose the narrow way, for a tree is known by its fruit, and some who cry 'Lord, Lord' will not enter the kingdom of heaven', so be wise builders and avoid those with foolish foundations (7; 1-27)

Matthew adds a footnote, after Jesus taught the disciples about kingdom ethics, for it appears that the crowds, who had followed Jesus and the disciples, were 'amazed at his teaching' because of his authority. The differences were so great that the people regarded Jesus as a greater teacher than the 'teachers of the law' (Matt. 7: 28-29). The witness, Matthew himself, does not say how many followed Jesus and his team, but such was the attraction of Jesus' ministry there must have been hundreds of followers (see Matt. 8: 1).

Reflection

Punk Monk, a book about 'new monasticism' takes the reader on a journey through a variety of routes that give pointers to a 'life of discipline.' It took me back to the time in theological college, when I was 'captured' by many pilgrimage stories of the Celtic 'saints.' I found Bede particularly interesting, mainly because he was based at the monastery of St.Paul, Jarrow. I found his disciplined lifestyle intoxicating – but too draconian - but he did challenge Celtic Christianity over 'thin places' and the veneration of saints, which in his eyes could lead to paganism. Certainly Bede and Punk Monk challenged me yet again, to be more disciplined in my own lifestyle. Jesus himself was deeply disciplined, kept time with his father sacrosanct, and lived a life full of joy in the Spirit, with the intention of building a dedicated team, to establish the church of God (Matt. 16: 18-19). In following Jesus, and or the Bede, the demand from both is that we are called to be spiritually fit. Basically, this includes the disciplines of prayer, fasting, meditation on Scripture, studying biblical material, living in the Spirit and sharing faith to the broken, wayward, captive peoples with the possibility of physical healing. To be like that calls for real faith.

Jesus taught 'other sermons' distinctly different from the sermon on the Mount or Plain. The other teaching given by Jesus in the Synoptics and John, is both complimentary and supplementary to the kingdom teaching in Matthew's Gospel (5: 1-7: 29). To call twelve men to leave their work and live with Jesus was a demand they could not refuse, so when he made the call, "Come, follow me" (Mk. 1: 17) there was only one response, 'they forsook all and followed him.' Being a disciple (Gk: mathetes) is about being a learner and the men were the 'inner core' of those willing to 'learn' from him (Mt. 11: 28-29). Jesus chose many topics to enrich his followers with the aim of advancing the kingdom of God. The following list is not exhaustive but does represent the width of Jesus' teaching approach: Obedience (Jn 14 23), Service (Jn. 13: 12-16), Love (Mt. 22: 37), Faith (Mk. 11: 22), Suffering (Mk. 8: 31 Mt. 16: 24-25), Church or Community (Mt. 16: 17-18), Prayer (Lk. 11: 5-10), Truth (8: 32), Power (Mt. 10: 1; Lk. 10: 20), Life (Lk. 9:6) Evil (Mt. 12: 35), Satan (Mt. 25: 41), Judgement (Mt. 12: 36), Hope (Mt. 11: 28-29) Inner purity (Mk. 7 1-23), Prophecy (Mk. 13: 14-20).

Jesus, the Messiah-King, taught parables to explain the kingdom to his disciples and hide the truth from the public. He heralded the Messianic Age for "the kingdom is among you" (Lk. 17: 21) here and now – you do not have to wait for some far off tomorrow – and yet it is still to come! There are between forty and sixty parables in the Gospels. The word 'parable' (Gk: parabola) may be used of a proverb, a riddle, a comparison, but at its heart the parable is a metaphor or allegory. The parable is a 'like' saying, "The kingdom of God is like a mustard Seed" (Mk. 4 30-32). They aim to invite the audience to change - to change ways of thinking and lifestyle. In some way they are also prophetic, because Jesus took the truths of the visible world to explain the truths of the invisible world. Jesus' parables surprise, shock, astonish and provoke. He used two methods when telling a parable:

he aimed to **conceal** 'the mystery of the kingdom ...'

(Mt. 13 13-15; Mk. 4 10-12) and

he sought to **reveal** the kingdom to those who had ears to hear.

He made much of the tension between the present and the future of the kingdom, with the first being about salvation and the second judgement, but both refer to one kingdom. The parables may be placed into three sections:

The Gospel of God – the Story of the kingdom

The examples are: The Sower, the Tares, the Mustard seed, the Leaven, the Hidden Treasure, the Pearl, the Net, the Pharisee, and Lost Son (Part 1).

The Grace of God – the Story of Redemption

The examples are: the Lost Sheep, the Lost Coin, the Lost Son (Part 2), the Good Samaritan, Two debtors, the Friend at Midnight.

The Glory of God – the Story of Hope

The examples are: the Fig Tree, the Ten Virgins, the Wedding Feast, the Great Banquet, the Wheat and the Weeds.

(Headings: The Parables, Robert Farrar Capon, E, 1988/9).

Three parables have been chosen illustrating each distinctive theme: the Gospel of God – the Mustard Seed, the Grace of God - the Lost Sheep and Coin, and the Glory of God - the Wedding Feast.

The Mustard Seed (Matt. 13: 31-32)

'The kingdom of heaven is like a mustard seed which a man took and planted in a field' (Matt. 13: 31). The 'seed' was one of the smallest known seeds but at some stage, this same seed would eventually become a great shrub that will allow birds to nestle in its branches. Jesus also linked the mustard seed to faith 'If you have faith as small as a mustard seed ... nothing will be impossible to you' (Matt. 17: 20). If the disciples had doubts about Jesus and the message of the kingdom, this was, for them, a word of encouragement because the kingdom, like the seed, will grow beyond recognition. This was a prophetic announcement and seems to be located in Daniel's vision of the 'tree' as an image of a great kingdom (Dan. 4: 10-12). The Daniel passage also pictures 'birds in its branches' representing nations gathered under protection of a great 'new' empire. It is clear that Jesus is including non-Jews (Gentiles) coming in to the kingdom of heaven for the kingdom is constantly expanding. The connection of the mustard seed with faith stimulates the disciples to see that such a 'tiny' faith will accomplish much that appears impossible.

Reflection

The teaching of Jesus on the mustard seed had a profound effect upon Count Nicholas Von Zinzendorf in the early 17th century. As a young man, Zinzendorf enthusiastically embraced the teachings of the Gospels. With some friends he had been involved in a revival, formed themselves into a group committed to deepening their spiritual relationship with Christ. In 1718, they met together in secret with each wearing a ring, which was engraved in Greek: 'None live for themselves.' They enjoyed praying, having fun, shared in breaking bread (the Eucharist), and formed the Mustard Seed. They covenanted together to:

> To be true to Christ
>
> To be kind to all people
>
> To spread the Gospel to the world.

They based their gatherings on the teaching of Jesus about loving God and loving their neighbour (Matt. 22: 37-40; 28: 18-20). Zinzendorf heard about the persecution of the Moravians and decided to let them have the use of land and property in Saxony. This decision had far-reaching implications for the growth and impact of the Gospel and

was really the start of the modern missionary movement:
- It led to a revival in 1727 known as the Moravian Pentecost.
- It resulted in a 24/7 prayer movement which lasted for a hundred years.
- It caused the Church to see that 'missions' was a 'cause celebre' in order to expand God's kingdom worldwide.

The Mustard Seed Covenant enshrined in the teaching of Jesus about the growth of the kingdom of God, and the faith exercised, brought radical change to the way Christians and Churches saw the missionary task. The kingdom of God was beginning to expand across the nations from generation to generation.

The Lost Sheep and Lost Coin (Luke 15: 1-10)

The setting of this set of parables – the Lost Sheep, the Lost Coin and the Lost Son (this last will not be used) provides an interesting background (Luke 15: 1-2). There are three groups of people listening to Jesus: a) the tax collectors, b) the sinners, and c) the Pharisees and Scribes. The first two groups were regarded as the 'lost' by the religious authorities who saw them as ungodly outcasts. No self-respecting Rabbi, like Jesus, would associate with such people. So the jibe that Jesus 'receives sinners and eats with them' (Luke 15: 2) was a put-down which showed he could not possibly be righteous for he, like them, was nothing more than a sinful man. Yet, the rejected are drawn to hear Jesus! Moreover, they drew close despite facing the truth about the cost of discipleship (Luke. 14: 25-27). There was a definite magnetism about Jesus. Ordinary people felt comfortable in his presence. His teaching was powerful and his actions were full of compassion to those in need. It would be true to say that the despised and disregarded felt 'at home' in the presence of such goodness.

    Jesus ignores his critics and tells the crowd about a pastoral scene, which would have been familiar to the crowd. A shepherd had a flock of one hundred sheep. It was common to count the numbers of sheep and this was done by calling them by name. Instead of a hundred, there were only ninety-nine – one was missing! A sheep was lost and had to be found, so the shepherd set about looking for the lost sheep. The shepherd finds the sheep, lifts it on his shoulder, and brings it back into the pen. A party follows as the shepherd shares his joy with his friends and neighbours, for 'I have found my sheep which was lost' (Luke 15: 6). In the same way, 'there will be joy in heaven over one person who repents than over the ninety-nine righteous persons who do not repent' (Luke 15: 7).

Jesus continues to reinforce the first story by describing a woman who owned ten silver coins, but in the course of the day, lost one (Luke 15: 8-10). She is distraught and searches her home, sweeping the floor and using a lamp to lighten her home until she finds the coin. The coin is probably a drachma – the equivalent to a day's wages – so it was very valuable for the woman. The lost coin is found. Again, as in the first story, Jesus announces, 'there is rejoicing in the presence of the angels over one who repents' (Luke 15: 10).

The Wedding Feast (Matt. 22: 1-14)

Some commentators have linked the Great Banquet with the Wedding Feast, and it is clear that there are similar elements in both stories. However, each parable is quiet distinct and each carries its own truth. 'The kingdom of heaven may be compared to a king who gave a wedding feast for his son, and sent his servants to call those who were invited to the wedding feast, but they would not come. Again, he sent other servants, saying 'Tell those who are invited, see, I have prepared my dinner, my oxen and my fat calves have been slaughtered, and everything is ready. Come to the wedding feast. But they paid no attention and went off, one to his farm, another to his business, while the rest seized his servants, treated them shamefully and killed them. The king was angry, sent his troops, destroyed the murderers, and burned their city. Then he said to his servants, 'The wedding feast is ready, but those I invited did not deserve to come. Go to the street corners and invite to the banquet anyone you find. Therefore, the servants went out into the streets and gathered all the people they could find, both good and bad, and the wedding hall filled up with guests. Nevertheless, when the king came in to see the guests, he noticed a man who was there who was not wearing wedding clothes. 'Friend,' he asked, 'how did you get in here without wedding clothes? The man was speechless. Then the king told the attendants:

> 'Bind him hand and foot and cast him into outer darkness. In that place, there will be weeping and gnashing of teeth. For many are invited but few are chosen' (Matt. 22: 1-14).

The whole tenor of this parable is about a great occasion at the 'end of the Age.' This time though, it is a wedding, which seems to represent the final Messianic Party in Glory. There will be a Day – a Day when the kingdom will be complete – that brings together those who will be part of this amazing gathering. To help us understand what Jesus is saying, the parable divides into three parts:

There is the Wedding Invitation (Matt. 55: 1-7).

This was no ordinary wedding – this is the wedding of the king's son – and as such the invites were to those who would join in the celebration. The Feast was ready and the table was set. The invites though, were rejected. None of the original recipients regarded the event as worth their attention. The history of Israel confirms that repeatedly when God sent out his servants to share the plan of God - there was little response. The prophets came: Moses, Samuel, David, Elijah, Elisha, Isaiah, Jeremiah, Daniel and many others. These servants of God were often treated with disdain. Some, according to Jesus' story, lost their lives. The justice of God was meted out and the city was destroyed. This 'prophetic' parable seems to hint at Jerusalem – the city of Zion, the centre of Israel's faith – being destroyed.

There is the Wedding Reception (Matt. 22: 8-10)

The king called his servants and with a great flourish and sent them out to 'call' the good and bad to come to the reception and join the feast. This is not a reference as such to righteousness and unrighteousness; rather it appears to speak of the weak and strong in society. Nor is this about believers and non-believers. Finally, the Wedding reception hall is full of guests. The party can now begin, for the chosen and called are present. This seems to be the highpoint of the story for everyone is gathered in and the son and guests can rejoice together. A minority of scholars see this parable as the Marriage Supper of the Lamb and the uniting of Christ (the Bridegroom) and Bride (the

Church) – but maybe that is taking this too far. There is, in the midst of the celebration, one last issue to deal with.

There is the Wedding Robe (Matt. 22: 14)

As the king views the guests he notices that there is a man present who is without a 'wedding garment' (Matt. 22; 11). He was improperly dressed and should not have been allowed into the celebration. When challenged, the man became speechless. Some argue that this robe is none other than the righteousness of Christ which is imputed and imparted to those who confess their sin, repent, and trust in the finished work of the Son of Man on the cross (Rom. 3: 25-26; 13: 14; Gal. 3: 27). The sad feature of the man without proper clothing means that he, having made his own choice, cannot be part of God's everlasting kingdom. Such a person will be placed in 'outer darkness' and there shall be 'weeping and grinding of teeth' (Matt. 8: 12; 13: 42; 24: 15). However this part of the parable is viewed, the picture is intended to confront the audience with the awfulness of rejecting the good news of the kingdom. In doing so, the outcome would appear to be permanent separation from God, thereby missing the final blessings of the New Age. Whatever else we say about the parable the teaching in the Wedding Feast, Jesus is allowing the crowd to think and reflect on the 'end in view.' The 'end' suggests a choice – either for or against Christ – there is no middle way nor, it would appear, is there some kind of second chance beyond death. For some there is everlasting bliss, while for others there is everlasting torment. Throughout his life and ministry, the Glory of God was present in Jesus, even when people did not see it or recognise it. He constantly referred to the future and the 'Final Day' when great events would happen when everyone will be confronted with the full Glory of the Messiah-King.

The composition of the parables, vary according to the setting and the audience Jesus found himself addressing. He chose stories that were always visual and tangible and he never attempted to mislead, confuse or manipulate his audience. It was this, combined with Jesus' authority through the Holy Spirit that made such an impact on the people, for there was always a response to his teaching – either positive or negative – for there was no middle way. "And this gospel of the kingdom will be preached in the whole world as a testimony to the nations, and then the end will come" (Mt. 24: 14). The teaching of the parables imply claims to the actual deity of Jesus:

> 'Jesus constantly linked himself to God
> Jesus demands acceptance or denial
> Jesus insists that his works are by the Spirit and not by Beelzebub
> Jesus divides his audiences into followers or enemies
> Jesus insists that there is no half-way house.'
> (Interpreting the Parables, Craig L. Blomberg, p. 326-327).

The Features of the Kingdom

Reflection

In London – things happen! That can be taken as read, but what happened next caused surprise and confusion. My wife and I were on a bus on a summer's day as it rolled along, heading for Croydon. We had decided to travel on the top deck – to look at places of memory – when a young Afro-Caribbean man appeared with Bible in hand. He announced his intention, opened his Bible, and began to share the gospel of the kingdom of God. We, the passengers, were the congregation. He shouted that Jesus had come to 'save us' and now was the moment to repent, confess Christ and receive forgiveness. He was lively, passionate, blunt but dynamic and made his plea – now was the time to step into God's kingdom. The audience were largely passive – but after ten minutes – he made an appeal and asked for a response. Silence! Then, trying again, offered to sit and chat. One passenger, about the same age, a Muslim, called him – he wanted to hear more. We were at our stop, so we departed to continue our journey. What a great moment – a God moment – when a young man, fired with a determination to preach Jesus – became an evangelist of the gospel of salvation. Whatever happened after that encounter, only eternity will know, but to see someone so spontaneous about their faith and so confident in the message, was a pleasure, joy and we offered thanks to Jesus! Hallelujah! The kingdom of God is ever present among us – thank God.

There are a huge number of books, articles and literature about the kingdom of God available to people today who want to research this topic. Often, when reading some of the materials the concept comes across abstractly. This is unfortunate because, however understood, one aspect stands out – the kingdom of God is dynamic. To crystallise what this means, the following features provide a balanced understanding of God's kingdom and how it affects people – believer and non-believer in every generation.

The kingdom of God has to be entered

No one enters the kingdom of God by his or her own will for God gives the kingdom and declares for whom it is for (Mt. 5 3). God provides it and compels humankind to enter it for 'all is now ready' (Mk. 10: 14; Lk 14: 15-24). The coming of the kingdom is a sovereign act of God. Jesus, with his disciples, urged men and women to search for it, seek it, find it and enter it by repentance, faith and grace for it was present among them (Mk. 10 15 Mt. 6: 19, 33). The coming of the kingdom was for the blessing of the multitudes, but basically it was for the salvation of humankind, and thus it was always good news (Mk. 1: 15). The offer included forgiveness, peace and joy for those who believed in the gospel. When Jesus introduced people to the reign of God, breaking Satan's control of their suffering and sin, an atmosphere of celebration resulted (Mk. 2: 1-12). The crowds, seeing people being set free, healed and delivered from demonic bondage, glorified God (Lk. 10: 17). To become disciples of Jesus and live the kingdom lifestyle, was to face persecution and hatred (Mt. 5: 11-12). Discipleship always costs because, whatever else it means, the reign of God was a complete reversal to the common standards of society and challenged the status quo.

The kingdom of God is relational

The basis of that relationship is belief in and experience of the 'work' of Christ and the 'word' of Christ. To repent and trust in Jesus as Saviour and Lord is to enter into an intimate personal relationship with the Messiah-King (Mt. 11: 28-29). To be a follower is to lose one's life in order to save it (Mt. 16: 24-25). The work of the Spirit brings about that inner change (Lk. 11: 13) and continues to work in and through the believer bringing transformation and assurance (Rom. 8: 17). The result of regeneration and sanctification confirms that such a person is a child of God in the kingdom of God. Such change and submission is expressed in worship (Lk. 10: 27; Acts 2: 4, 11), love (Mk. 14: 6-9), prayer (Mt. 6: 9-13) and service (Mt. 9: 37 10: 8).

The kingdom of God is Mysterious

Essentially, the kingdom of God is secretive, subversive and eternal. It can seem, at times, to be like an early morning mist – it is there and then it is gone! The kingdom cannot be controlled, because it is the intention of God to grow and advance his kingdom. Jesus in his teaching often preached about the kingdom being present and future (Mk. 10: 30). Certainly, the kingdom had arrived in Jesus, the Messiah-King. One sign of that is Jesus casting out demons for the 'kingdom of heaven has been forcefully advancing' or 'coming violently' (Mt. 11: 12; Mk. 3: 21-27; Mt. 12: 28). But Jesus also taught his disciples that that the kingdom will come at the end of the age (Mt. 24: 1-25: 28). This is sometimes referred to as the 'now' and 'not yet' of the kingdom of God. Nicodemus, the Pharisee and theologian, in his conversation with Jesus, found the whole conversation disturbing and puzzling. For Jesus informed him that he had to become like a child, to enter God's kingdom. To be 'reborn' in order to enter the kingdom was too mysterious for the Rabbi. Jesus intimated to another doubter that "My kingdom is not of this world ..." (Jn. 18 36). It is through the Spirit that the rule and reign of God becomes known and experienced. Yet, the people of the kingdom and the people beyond the kingdom, like the sheep and the goats, will be mixed together until the end time takes place. Even though the arrival of the kingdom is small, like the mustard seed, for one day it will fill the whole world with leaven, for it is like treasure or a priceless pearl. Jesus put it bluntly:

> "seek first the kingdom of God and his righteousness, and all these things will be given to you ..." (Mt. 6 33).

In other words, choose the kingdom now and prepare for the final kingdom when it arrives (Rev. 11: 15).

The Kingdom of God and the Church

The church is not synonymous with the kingdom. The church is the community of the kingdom but is not the community itself. The kingdom is greater than the church. The church cannot produce the kingdom, but as the church proclaims the kingdom – it brings the kingdom to the people. Ladd makes some interesting observations:

> The kingdom creates the church
>
> The church witnesses the kingdom
>
> The church is the instrument of the kingdom
>
> The church is the custodian of the kingdom
>
> (G E Ladd A Theology of the New Testament, 1979, 336-7).

The church provides a central place in God's redemptive purpose for humankind. Entering the kingdom is to enter into a saving relationship with Christ. The confession of Peter at Caesarea Philippi that Jesus was the Christ, resulted in the disciple being declared the rock on which the church would be built (Mt. 16: 17-19). The church, by proclaiming the presence of the kingdom of God, performed the 'works of Jesus' resulting in salvation, healing the sick and casting out devils to the glory of God (Mt. 10: 8; Lk. 10: 17). Having experienced God's reign, the church is the fellowship of those who have entered into the blessings of the new age, The government of God is not limited to the church for God's sovereign rule extends into the heavens, planet earth and even beneath terra firma (Phil. 2: 10; Col. 1: 15-20; Ps. 24: 1 Dan. 7: 27).

The kingdom of God will always Grow

Jesus expected the kingdom of God to grow. He spoke about God's reign extending across peoples and nations until the promised kingdom arrived (Mk.4: 26-32) The growth of the kingdom is the progressive reign over all God's creation and creatures. Central to this growth is the constant battle between the kingdom of God and the kingdom of darkness. This battle works itself out in the lives of the people for 'the kingdom is within' (Lk. 17: 21). For Jesus, the kingdom was a hidden reality but will, at some point, become known (Mt. 4: 17; 10: 7). The kingdom is proclaimed by kingdom people (Mt. 24: 14 Lk. 4: 17). The kingdom is pictured as being small – in its beginnings – but will spread and become huge, as in the mustard seed (Mt. 13: 31-33). It is also like yeast which works undercover and subverts the untruths of Satanic influences (Lk. 14: 33; Mk. 4: 3-8). Jesus uses other images of the kingdom expanding and growing (Mt. 13: 33 Lk. 14: 34; Mt. 5: 14; 13 47-48; Lk. 14: 21-24).

The Kingdom of God and the Spirit

One of the odd features of Christian literature is the way there is often a disconnection between some theological themes. For example, some books on Christian growth appear without any mention of the Holy Spirit. The same is also true, when it comes to the kingdom and the Holy Spirit. This is very unfortunate because these themes are so entwined together, so to separate them is to do a disservice to the reader. The Gospels portray Jesus, not only as one with the Father and the Spirit – the Trinity – but also as the Son of God and Son of Man, who taught at a level and depth beyond any other teacher. The uniqueness of Jesus' teaching is centred in that wholesome relationship. The radical upbringing of Jesus, in the home of Mary and Joseph, and his time in the synagogue learning the Scriptures, was fundamental to his future ministry. Throughout his life from birth to resurrection, the Holy Spirit never left Jesus. His birth, circumcision, early life and baptism tell the story of someone engulfed in the Spirit, which was confirmed by his anointing at his baptism in the river Jordan (Mt. 3: 13-17 Mk. 1 9-13; Lk. 3 21-23). This anointing by the Spirit is referred to by Jesus in the synagogue in Nazareth, when he reads from the Isaiah scroll:

"The Spirit of the Lord is on me because he has anointed me to preach ... to proclaim ..." (Isa. 61: 1-2; Lk. 4: 16-21). In other words, Jesus' authoritative teaching ministry was the outcome of his anointing by the Spirit at his baptism. John's Gospel contains a remarkable tribute to Jesus by his cousin, John the Baptist, "For he whom God has sent utters the words of God, for he gives the Spirit without limit" (John 3: 34).

The Kingdom of God at War

Any reading of the Gospels and the Acts of the Apostles, brings to the fore the constant battle between the forces of goodness and the forces of darkness (Lk. 4: 25-29; 11: 14-20; Acts 4: 18-22; 10 37=38). Indicative of the coming conflict began at the start of Jesus' ministry when he was anointed (Mt. 3: 16-17), and immediately faced an onslaught on his person and ministry from evil powers in the person of Satan (Mt. 4: 1-11). That initial fight with its threefold attack: a) dismissing Jesus' claim to be the Son of God (twice), b) dragging Jesus to the pinnacle of the temple to ask for the security of the angelic host should he throw himself off the temple, c) offering Jesus the kingdoms of the world if he would only worship Satan. To the three temptations Jesus reacted by quoting from the Scriptures: a) man lives by every word that comes from the mouth of God Deut. 8: 3), b) do not tempt the Lord your God (Deut. 6: 16), c) and worship the Lord your God, and serve him only (Deut. 6: 13). The battle royal, between Jesus and Satan, over a period of 40 days and nights, was constantly intense hour after hour with no let up with the temptations repeated, in all probability hundreds of times. After such an onslaught Jesus, the Son of God, must have been exhausted, emotionally and physically, no wonder he received the welcome attention of an angelic team of angels who ministered to him (Mt. 4: 11). That initial encounter set the scene for the ongoing conflict that would pursue Jesus throughout his ministry, even up to his death on a Roman gibbet, with crowds mocking, swearing, laughing, and denying that he was the Messiah, until he died the death of deaths (Mt. 27 32-50). Yet, what appeared as defeat was but a prelude to victory 'as up from the grave He arose, a mighty triumph o'er his foes' for out of his resurrection salvation was secure, and the King and his kingdom were victorious (Mk. 16: 6; Rom. 1: 4).

Reflection

In the last week of his ministry, Jesus taught his disciples that they would face onslaughts from evil and the forces of darkness, 'But stay awake at all times, praying that you may have strength to escape all these things that are going to take place, and stand before the Son of Man' (Luke 21: 36). There's a war to be faced, and Jesus was insistent that the disciples prepare for the days when they would face greater satanic activity. John Piper, writing nearly thirty years ago wrote:

'We simply must seek for ourselves and our people a wartime mentality ... until we feel the desperation of a wartime bombing raid, or the thrill of a new strategic offensive for the gospel, we will not pray in the Spirit of Jesus. The crying need of the hour is to put churches on a wartime footing' (John Piper, Let the Nations be Glad, IVF, 47-48).

The first part of the kingdom prayer is importunate – pleading, asking, demanding – 'Our Father in heaven hallowed be your name. Your kingdom come, your will be done, on earth as it is in heaven' (Matt. 6: 9-10). Crying, singing, shouting such prayer, links with the global 24/7 prayer movement which has raised the spectrum of prayer to a new level. Although the levels of prayer has dropped in the UK, there is no doubt that directive, demanding prayer is what is required from today's churches.

The mission of Jesus focused on the good news of the gospel of the kingdom, which included setting people free from captive forces. The opening chapters of Mark's Gospel (1-5), gives an insight into the combative nature of the war Jesus waged against the powers of darkness, evil and Satan and we are called to follow suit. The following list provides a selective number of those transformed by the good news of the kingdom:

- an evil spirit is driven out of a man in the synagogue in Capernaum
- the mother-in-law of one of the disciples is healed
- a leper is restored and cleansed of leprosy
- a paralysed man is healed of his paralysis
- a man's shrivelled hand is completely restored
- a demon-possessed man is set free
- a woman with a haemorrhage is healed
- a daughter is raised from the dead (Mk. 1: 13-5: 43).

Other miraculous events take place with the calming of the storm on Galilee, the feeding of the 5,000 and the 4,000, and then to the amazement of the disciples, Jesus walks on water (Mk. 6: 44; 8: 9; Lk. 8: 24; Mt. 14. 25). Apart from the healing miracles, time and again Jesus gave people hope for their souls, as well as their bodies, because only he could offer forgiveness of sins ((Mark 2: 9; Matt. 9: 4; Mark 11: 25).

Added to these incidents are the times when Jesus is verbally accosted, criticised and falsely accused of blasphemy against God. His announcement of the arrival of the 'new age' of the kingdom, provoked fury with the devil and all hell broke loose against the Son of Man. There is no question but that the reactions of the authorities to Jesus and his subsequent betrayal, arrest, interrogation, trials, torture and crucifixion was motivated by Satanic influences (Judas included, Mt. 26 49). Jesus' response is put in the form of a future event: "Shall not God avenge his own elect who cry out day and night to him, though he bares long with them? I tell you the truth that he will avenge them speedily. Nevertheless, when the Son of Man comes, will he find faith on the earth" (Lk. 18: 6-8). The implication is that there will certainly be faith, kingdom faith, on the earth. This battle does not end with Jesus death on the cross, but when the final curtain comes down at the end of time. Then, the battle, the conflict, and the war will be over for Jesus will be seen as the victor over death, disease, sin and Satan (Rev. 1: 4-8; 19: 1-22-22: 21). One scholar summarises Jesus view of the ages:

"In brief, this age, which extends from creation to the Day of the Lord ... is the age of human existence, and weakness and mortality, of evil, sin and death. The Age to come will see a realisation of all that the reign of God means, and will be the age of resurrection into eternal life in the kingdom of God. Everything in the Gospels points to the idea that life in the kingdom of God in the 'Age to Come' will be life on earth – but life transformed by the kingly rule of God when his people enter into the ... divine blessings " (Mt. 19: 28).

(A Theology of the New Testament, G E Ladd, p. 48).

The Two Kingdoms

It is true that the emphasis in the New Testament speaks plainly of one kingdom – the kingdom of God, and does not explicitly refer to the devil and his minions as a 'kingdom.' However, it is also clear that the existence of sin, death, disease and a personal devil exists, and placing their activity under the word 'kingdom' helps us to recognise the nature of the conflict we face and are engaged in. Two biblical scenes, one from the Old Testament and one from the New Testament, remind believers that conflict, spiritual warfare faces every generation of believers.

Scene 1 is from the book of Joshua:

"Now when Joshua was near Jericho, he ... saw a man standing in front of him with drawn sword in his hand" and asked, Are you for us or for our enemies?" (Josh. 5: 13). The man assured Joshua that he was "the commander of the Lord's army" at which point the Patriarch "fell face down to the ground in reverence" and took off his "sandals, for the place where you are standing is holy" for the "Lord will deliver Jericho into your hands"(Josh. 5: 15, 6: 2). The battle for the Promised Land was about to start, with a triumphant victory under the direct leadership of the Lord.

Scene 2 is from the book of Hebrews:

"Therefore, since we are surrounded by so great a cloud of witnesses ... let us lay aside every weight, and sin ... looking to Jesus, the founder and perfected of our faith ..." (Heb. 12: 1-2). The "cloud of witnesses" refers to Old Testament saints like Abel, Enoch, Noah, Abraham and Sarah, Moses as well as unnumbered heroes and heroines who "overthrew kingdoms, established justice and gained what was promised" (Heb. 11: 17-25 et. al). Others, New Testament saints (1st Christians), were constantly attacked who faced torture, were beaten, imprisoned for "They were stoned to death ... sawn in two ... put to the sword ... deprived, oppressed, ill-treated" (Heb. 11: 33-37).

True, the term 'spiritual warfare' is not used of either group, but whereas the first depended upon Yahweh, the second kept their "eyes fixed on Jesus" but both groups faced conflict. Above all, the kingdom of God has come for the kingdom is 'upon you' and 'within you' (Matt. 12: 28). Accordingly, Jesus' own revelation that the kingdom of God had come in him, was a time-honoured God moment (Mark 1: 14; Luke 4: 43). The graphic breaks it down for

THE KINGDOM OF LIGHT →	← THE KINGDOM OF DARKNESS
The Government of God	**The Chaos of Satan**
Light	Darkness
Salvation	Bondage to sin
Healing	Disease
Deliverance	Evil spirits
Miracles	Disaster
Truth	Lies
Peace	War

Unity	Disunity
Resurrection	Death

We could add to the lists, but they represent some of the characteristics of two distinct kingdoms battling for supremacy over humankind. Thankfully, despite what often appears to the contrary, the kingdom of God ultimately triumphs over the kingdom of darkness. The 'power struggle' is, in a real sense, a fight to the death. In essence, it is a battle – a war – between God and Satan, the Church and the world, and the Spirit and the flesh. This spiritual war is a constant and will continue until the consummation of all things. In the meantime, believers would benefit from being aware of the invisible spiritual forces that are controlled by an evil and powerful enemy. Jesus himself faced battle after battle with the powers of darkness throughout his life and contended:

"If I drive out demons by the finger of God then the kingdom of God has come upon you" (Lk. 14: 29-31). One significant story is the deliverance of Legion from the power of the 'evil one.' In meeting the 'possessed man' Jesus used two commands to release the man from his captivity: a) he cast out the evil spirits from the man and b) demanded the man's name (Lk. 8: 29-31). Through Jesus' ministry, the kingdom of God arrived – the reign of God prevailed – and the man was freed. In encouraging the disciples to be involved in such a ministry, Jesus was introducing them into the conflict between God and Satan. The disciples had to learn that, unlike Jesus, they may meet failure (Mt. 17 14-16), and so were reminded that "faith, prayer and fasting" were foundational principles to setting people free from any form of evil control for "if you have faith ... nothing will be impossible for you" (Mt. 17: 17-20). Nevertheless, when Jesus sent out seventy to minister, they rejoiced when they returned because "even the demons are subject to us in your name" (Lk. 10: 17). For them, the truth was not to boast about their success, but to rejoice "that their names were written in heaven" (Lk. 10: 20).

Reflection

In today's churches, particularly in the West, there are still debates over the ministry of healing and the casting out of evil spirits. There is little disagreement among bible teachers over the healing ministry of Jesus and the disciples. Such accounts in the Gospels and Acts are accepted as authentic by the majority of commentators. The difficulty arises when it comes to 'acting out' such a ministry in the modern world. It is not that healings and miracles do not take place – they do. But here, sadly, there are churches who dismiss claims or ignore facts even when confirmed by medical practitioners. There is, however, a growing number of church leaders who believe such a ministry should be a feature of the evangelistic and prophetic work of the local church. In others words, proclamation and demonstration belong together. Faith sharing that leaves out the prospect of healing and the miraculous goes against the teaching and practice of Jesus, the disciples and the Early Church (Mt. 9: 35-10: 1-42; 28: 16-20; Mk. 16: 15-20; Acts 3: 1-16; 4: 23-31). It has been calculated that 727 verses in the Gospels relate specifically to saving and healing physical, mental and emotional illnesses and, on occasions, raising people from the dead. In reading through the Gospels some 70 people appear to have been freed from evil spirits. Similarly, the Acts of the Apostles covering a period of 30 years, contain specific supernatural conversions, miraculous incidents, signs and wonders, the casting out of evil spirits and raising the dead. Thankfully, there is plenty of evidence to confirm miraculous healings in the developing world, confirmed by medics and missionaries working in those fields. Perhaps it is time, not just to talk about such a 'gospel ministry of healing' but to practice such a ministry in our communities. The Good News is much wider than 'saving souls' for the word salvation (soteria) includes the whole being of a person – spirit, mind and body. Peter, speaking to the Sanhedrin is explicit when he says, "Salvation/healing (soteria) is found in no else, for there is no other name under heaven given to men by which we must be saved/healed (sothenai)" (Acts 4: 12).

In terms of its efficacious work, that one act of redeeming love, was set in the 'now' time with a view to the 'then' time! This refers, of course, to the 'already' and the 'not yet' of the kingdom. The kingdom of God is centred on Jesus in his person and work, through supernatural salvation and the eternal coming kingdom. For instance, when someone is saved or healed it is the age of the future coming into the present age, but at some date in the future, that person will die physically. In other words, the kingdom has come - and is present – but the kingdom will come in all its fullness at some stage in the future. Bible teachers refer to this as the consummation of the kingdom of God. The kingdom of God is found in the life, teaching, and action of Jesus and is present for salvation and judgment now. A new day of God's rule has dawned, with all its implications for human life. With others we rejoice in the coming of the kingdom, which brings salvation; the blessings of the new age in Christ; and with the prospect of the coming of the kingdom of God, to the glory of God the Father (MT. 24: 30-31; Jn. 17: 20-23).

Signs of the Kingdom

The signs of the kingdom are rampant in the Gospels and clearly emphasise the sovereignty, authority and power of God. The redemptive reign of God had become dynamically present in history. In the Synoptic story, the term 'kingdom of God' (Hb: malkuth; Gk: basileia) is used 121 times, and the 'kingdom of heaven' 33 times. The writers consistently point to the ministry of Jesus in terms of the advance of the kingdom: "Jesus went through all the towns and villages, teaching in their synagogues, preaching the good news and healing every disease and sickness" (Mt. 4: 23-25; 9: 35; Mk. 1: 32-34; Lk. 4: 43; 8: 1; 9: 11). Four basic meanings of the word 'kingdom' can be found in the Gospels:

- It is the reign or rule of God;
- It is a future apocalyptic world into which the righteous enter at the end of the age;
- It is the presence of the kingdom which will release his power in the world;
- It is a present realm or sphere into which people enter (G.E. Ladd, Jesus and the Kingdom).

John and Jesus preached about the reign of God through repentance and baptism, which resulted in salvation. The good news is more than coming under the authority of Jesus, with the disciples and later the church, engaging in a ministry of change and transformation as the kingdom of God manifested itself in society. The signs of the kingdom are seen in the 'works' of Jesus. Each of the Gospels contains descriptions of incidents in which supernatural activity takes place. The eyewitness gospel accounts simply record what was seen and heard though, what we have in the narratives, is but a summary of Jesus' hands-on-ministry:

> "Jesus did many other miraculous signs in the presence of his disciples which are not recorded in this book. But these are written that you may believe that Jesus is the Christ, the Son of God, and that by believing you may have life in his name" (Jn. 20: 30-31). What was true of John's witness is equally true of the Synoptic Gospels.

Throughout his short ministry, Jesus was at the centre of the kingdom message. When a moment of controversy arose between the disciples as to who Jesus really was, he pointed them to his 'works' (Gk: erga): "Believe me when I say that I am in the Father and the Father is in me, or at least believe on the evidence of the miracles themselves" (Jn. 14: 11). The works or miracles of Jesus may be summarised from a familiar passage:

> Preaching the gospel of the kingdom of God
>
> Proclaiming release for the captives
>
> Liberating those who are in bondage
>
> Inaugurating the year of Jubilee (Lk. 4: 18-19).

Jesus explains that the purpose of his coming is to bring salvation by setting people free from sin, disease and Satan. By referring to the 'year of jubilee' (Isa. 61: 1-3) Jesus was proclaiming that the 'year of the Lord's favour' had arrived, which meant that debts were cancelled and slaves were freed. That provocative picture, announced in the synagogue of Nazareth was a message of hope for the needy in society.

In a word, he was the 'eschatological prophet' announcing the arrival of a new age, which would bring salvation, healings and miracles. For instance, salvation results from the actions of Jesus and brings dramatic change: "Today salvation has come to your house (Zacchaeus) ... for the Son of Man came to seek and save the lost" (Lk. 19: 9-10). In speaking as he did, Jesus was re-enforcing the fact that his preaching and teaching, was the message of the Father (Jn. 14: 10). He made it clear in the 'Disciples Prayer' that as they pray to the Father the kingdom will be done on earth as it is in heaven (Mt. 6: 9).

The Kingdom of God and Ministry

The dynamic nature of the kingdom of God is demonstrated through its ministry to people with spiritual, physical, emotional needs. Ministry is a wholesome approach to humanity, in that it takes into account both the message and the methods by which the good news is proclaimed and demonstrated. This was true of Jesus and the disciples, and the apostolic leaders in the Early Church. The telling of the story was always mission-hearted. The Great Commandment and the Great Commission belong together, and are the bedrock of church activity towards a wayward and wicked world (Mt. 22: 37-39; 28: 18-20). The ultimate goal of mission is that "every tongue should confess that Jesus Christ is Lord, to the glory of God the Father" (Phil. 2: 11). Running alongside the evangelism of the church, is a prophetic note of both the present and the future dimensions of the kingdom. Prophetic insights are fundamental to the survival and development of the church and the growth of God's kingdom. There are therefore, two distinct and yet complementary features of relational and generational ministry: i) Evangelism and ii) Prophecy.

The Evangelistic Role

The preaching, teaching and healing ministry of Jesus contain the double thrust of reproduction and multiplication (Mk. 1: 15; 4: 20). Two words dominate gospel communication, witness (Gk: marturia) and proclamation (Gk: kerygma). The first is about being willing to give one's life for the good news and the second is about proclaiming the word of the good news. The evangelistic task is to make certain the good news of kingdom-salvation in Jesus Christ, is proclaimed to the world of humanity and is witnessed to by disciples in every generation. This means that:

- the priority in gospel evangelism is the glory of God
- the sharing of the gospel witness is always personal and corporate
- the communication of the gospel is both proclamation and demonstration
- the outcome of faith-sharing is the formation of the Christian community
- the dynamic that brings about gospel transformation is the Holy Spirit
- the preservation of the gospel community is through worship, prayer, fellowship and discipleship.

The Prophetic Role

Prophecy is understood in various ways in the Scriptures. In both Testaments, prophetic announcements are used to make clear God's intentions for an individual or a community. Such prophetic words are often accompanied by signs and wonders that confirm the words spoken. The gift of prophecy is given for the purpose of providing direction for the evangelistic thrust, and the growth of the church in the present or the future: This highlights important truths:

- prophecy is a work of the Holy Spirit
- prophecy gives direction to a community of believers
- prophecy motivates changes that are necessary for God's work to expand
- prophecy enhances the unity of the community
- prophecy confirms the significance of the preached word and deed.

Evangelism and prophecy are gifts given by God to establish the kingdom through the church community and enrich its life. The purpose of such gifting is not only to grow the church but also to extend the kingdom and bring 'many sons and daughters to glory.' The gifting is for the blessing of humankind through the salvation of men and women in every generation.

Throughout this overview of the kingdom of God, the sovereign action of God has occurred throughout the Scriptures of the Old and New Testaments. The biblical documents are insistent that our sovereign Lord is in charge of the cosmos and humankind; for his purpose will be fulfilled in his time with a view to eternity. The coming of the kingdom – the rule or reign of God over all the previous ages – does not seem to hold sway. There appear to be too many variables through the evils of human hearts, and the constant interference of the powers of darkness. Yet, even in acknowledging that, the periods of the upsurge of evil and wickedness across the nations, continents and peoples, the final outcome will be the creation of a new order. One significant biblical example is to be found in a Psalm confirmed in the later chapters of Isaiah's prophecy: "Let this be written for a future generation, that a people not yet created may praise the Lord" (Ps. 102: 18). Such a generation, not yet born, is pictured as 'a broken, and despised people', who are a rescued and released humanity who will inhabit Zion, the New Jerusalem, full of praise "when the kingdoms assemble to worship the Lord" (Ps. 102: 19-22). Prophetically:

> "For Zion's sake I will not keep silent, for Jerusalem's sake I will not keep quiet, till her righteousness shines out like the dawn, salvation like a blazing torch, ... for the Lord has made proclamation to the ends of the earth: ... they will be called a holy people, the redeemed of the Lord ..."

The apostle's Peter and Paul catch the revelatory understanding in their Letters when writing about a 'new' day: "... you are a chosen people, a royal priesthood, a holy nation, a people belonging to God, that you may declare the praises of him who called you out of darkness into his wonderful light" (1 Pet. 2: 9). Likewise, Paul writes about a new generation, "If anyone is in Christ, he is a new creation: the old had gone, the new has come" (2 Cor. 5: 17). A new world is coming with a new humanity – different from the first humanity (Genesis 1-3) – in a renewed universe, in a new heavens and earth. Jesus was insistent that the 'final' kingdom would come in God's good time:

"Nation will rise against nation, and kingdom against kingdom. There will be earthquakes, famines, ...fearful events, and great signs from heaven. However, before all this, they will lay hands on you and persecute you ... on account of my name. There will be great distress ... until the times of the Gentiles will be fulfilled. There will be signs in the sun, moon and stars... At that time, they will see the Son of Man coming in a cloud with power and great glory. When you see these things begin to take place, stand up and lift up your heads, because your redemption is drawing near" (Lk. 21: 10-11, 23-28).

PART 2
Celebrating the Spirit's Ministry – in the Gospels

The four Gospels provide a panoramic view and biography of the life, ministry, death and resurrection of Jesus. The fulfilment of inductive prophecy recorded in the Old Testament is found in the gospel events in the New Testament. The opening words of the Gospel of Mark sets the tone for the gospel ministry of Jesus, "The beginning of the gospel of Jesus Christ, the Son of God" (Mark 1: 1 ESV). However Mark's Gospel emerged, and it is generally regarded as the first Gospel to be written, it's as if he could not get it out quickly enough to the believing community. The older English translations seem to back this up, for throughout his Gospel the word 'immediately' is used constantly. He is obviously impatient and wants the 'story of Jesus' to be released to those who are in the churches and communities in Palestine. For him, the Son of God had arrived and a new fresh age was present among the people. He pictures the scene by being a witness to John the Baptist, Jesus' cousin, and Jesus' baptism in the Jordan by John, resulting in Jesus receiving the Spirit's anointing. Within the space of a few words, Mark set the standard for the other gospel authors, for the key to Jesus' ministry is to be found in his baptism in the Holy Spirit. The proclamation of the 'kerugma' – the redemptive gospel words – will be demonstrated through the works of Jesus. His Gospel portrays, as do the other Gospels, one fact that is clear, that all the teachings, activities, events, and incidents in the life of Jesus come through the ministry of the Spirit. Each Gospel refers again and again to the supernatural nature of the ministry of Jesus throughout his short physical life on earth. The whole life of Jesus is evidenced by the presence and activity of the Holy Spirit. Jesus, the divine Son was one person, yet was both fully God and Man and that is a profound mystery we will never fully understand. Though, fully divine and fully human, he could only do the 'words and works' of the Father by being 'full' of the Spirit.

The actual presence of his incarnate birth and later his crucifying death show us:

- one of the great truths of the gospel is the kingdom of God
- what God is like and only Jesus can reconcile us to God
- that wayward humanity can be transformed
- what it is to be truly human
- that the more godly we are the more human we become
- helps us to have a life of worship, faith and witness.

> (M. Lloyd, [redacted] Cafe' Theology, A, 2005, 129ff.)

The Four Gospels

The Greek word 'pneuma' can mean 'wind' or 'breath' which is also used of 'unclean spirits' referring to demonic powers. I have chosen to keep to the terms 'the Holy Spirit' or 'the Spirit' or 'Spirit of God' which are references for the power and presence of God in action.

> One writer catches the mood of the narratives when he writes: 'In a universe where the footprints of God can be discerned in the heavens above and on the earth beneath, in human history and in personal experience, the most transparent testimony to God remains the Bible, the heart of which is the revelation of God in Jesus Christ our Lord. This witness reaches its clearest expression in the ... writings of the New Testament – the four Gospels ...' (The Making of the New Testament AGP, GR Beasley-Murray, A, 1992, 12)

The Gospels, as we have them, were written by anonymous men, in that for about the first fifty years, they were collections or records of the life, ministry, teaching and action of Jesus up to his death and resurrection. The names of the authors were attached some years later. The emergence of the manuscripts was probably a time of great joy for the early believers and, of course, the material did not emerge at the same time. What is significant is that these writings, when they appeared, gave a combined and compulsive understanding of the appearance of the Messiah-King in the 1st century AD. It is with this in mind that the four gospels provide us with a remarkable account of

God in action – Father, Son and Holy Spirit. There are about sixty plus recorded references to the way the Spirit acted during this early period in the lives of Jesus, the apostles and the people. The interjections that appear in the text, speak volumes of the way God acted through the Third Person of the Trinity. The people were 'amazed' 'astonished' 'dumfounded' 'speechless' 'awed' or 'we have seen remarkable things' depending on which translation is referred to. If we believe that, and we do, then the writers were under that same Spirit when they came to put together the actual textual matter. What we do have is a remarkable collection of God directed books (MSS) – pointing clearly to the coming, arrival and presence of God's one and only Son. To take the Bible or the textual material of the Scriptures for granted is a cardinal sin.

We would do well to remember what Jesus said about the Spirit, when speaking to a Jewish Rabbi, 'The wind blows wherever it pleases. You hear its sound, but you cannot tell where it comes from or where it is going. So it is with everyone born of the Spirit' (John 3: 8). The Spirit not only confirms who Jesus is, he also inspires his teaching and, to a limited degree, is involved in miraculous phenomenon, and supernatural physical healings. Jesus, as we have already intimated, lived and walked in the Spirit, and it was by and through the Spirit that he was enabled to bring about transformation in body, mind and soul. We will be looking at the following four books:

The four Gospels, Matthew, Mark, Luke and John are all biographies of Jesus. They tell the story of his life, his ministry of the miraculous, and the death and resurrection of Jesus, but the four records are not just historical for they speak about someone who is alive today. They were written to convince readers that he not only saved people then, he saves people in every time frame. The four Gospels consistently refer to Jesus as the Son of God, with the offer of eternal life to those who repent and believe. The first three Gospels are similar and have been described as a photo album, whereas John's Gospel is like a portrait. What is unusual about the four books is that they spend a good deal of their time writing about the last week in Jesus' life. Normally, biographies spend most of their time on the person's life, with a shorter time on the end of life. For Jesus, and those who read his story, it is the end of his life that makes sense of his earlier life.

Obviously, where the material from each Gospel is linked to other gospel materials we will include them together where possible. This is not going to be done slavishly, but some textual matter may dominate due to the nature of that material, and the person or persons involved. It is to be hoped that you find this helpful as we examine the textual data about the Spirit in the Gospels:

THE SPIRIT ▶ IN THE ▶ GOSPELS

- The Spirit and Prophetic announcements
- The Spirit and the Birth of Jesus
- The Spirit and John the Baptist
- The Spirit and Jesus' Baptism
- The Spirit and Jesus' ministry in the wilderness
- The Spirit and Spiritual darkness
- The Spirit Empowers Jesus to proclaim the Gospel
- The Spirit of Joy and Prayer
- The Spirit and Salvation
- The Spirit and Worship
- The Spirit and the Counsellor
- The Spirit and the Mission of the Church

The list of headings give an overview of the way the Holy Spirit acted in and through individuals. The twelve headings are simply a convenience to allow readers an overview of Spirit in the four Gospels. Considerable time has been given to the earlier part of this because they provide the foundations for the ministry of Jesus and the disciples. The 'building blocks' that make up the foundations are:

- ➢ The prophetic announcements
- ➢ The Birth of Jesus
- ➢ The anointing of Jesus for his life-work

- The temptations of Jesus in the wilderness
- The purpose of Jesus' ministry – salvation.
- The Spirit and Prophecy

Each of the four Gospels, in their opening sections, refer to John the cousin of Jesus who became known as the Baptist. For over four hundred years there had been no clear prophetic voice in Israel, but God suddenly speaks to an elderly childless couple, Zechariah and Elizabeth. Both were righteous and served and observed all the Lord's commands and decrees faultlessly. Zechariah was a priest who was a 'servant of order' in the Temple and, chosen by lot, ended up burning incense, and assembling the worshippers for worship and prayer (Luke 1: 6-10).. It was as he was doing his priestly duty that he was confronted by the angel Gabriel with a proclamation:

> 'Zechariah; your prayer has been heard. Your wife Elizabeth will have a son, John by name ... he will be great in the sight of the Lord. He will never take wine and he will be filled with the Holy Spirit even before he is born ... and he will go on before the Lord in the Spirit and power of Elijah ... to make ready a people prepared for the Lord' (Luke 1: 11-17).

The priest, scared by such an intervention and doubting and disbelieving the angel's prophecy, was struck dumb for his lack of faith (Luke 1: 20). Time moves on and Elizabeth, now pregnant, reaches the end of her term and her only child is born. As was the custom, he was taken by his parents to be circumcised and named. Elizabeth named the child John, an unusual family name but Zechariah still dumb, when asked by signs to name the child, named him John! Immediately, the father could speak and he, like his wife confirmed the name of their child. There was a time of thanksgiving – a berakah – with family and friends awestruck by all that had taken place, wondering what kind of person John would become (Luke 1: 57-66).

After the promise of a child, and the birth of John, his father Zechariah, filled with the Holy Spirit, burst into song. It could be that he was 'singing in the Spirit,' as he gave thanks for his son's birth, and prophetically saw the message of salvation being announced through his offspring, in which justice, holiness and righteousness would prevail: 'And you my child will be called a prophet of the Most High; for you will go on before the Lord to prepare the way for him' (Luke 1:1). As a consequence of the birth of John, there will be better days ahead for the nation (Luke 1: 67-79). John was to be the 'voice' – the voice of God, who will be preaching in the Spirit to the people declaring the coming of a greater person than he, for he was but a forerunner. More than that, he was to be akin to Elijah the prophet who, in the 9th cen. BC, was a feisty travelling prophet. As a prophet he challenged the status quo, and faced kings and people with the word of the Lord, The Spirit and power of Elijah was such that miracles happened, for a drought took place, foreign Baal deities and their followers were defeated on Mount Carmel, and he was taken up to heaven in a chariot of fire (1 Kings 18: 1-39; 2 Kings 2: 1-12).

Dramatically, John was to be the '2nd Elijah' (Mal.4: 5-6), whose preaching of repentance for sin and water baptism as a sign of forgiveness, announced the coming of the kingdom of heaven or God (Matt 3: 5-6; Mark 4: 26). His greatest message was that the coming of the Messiah was near (Matt. 3: 11-12). All the way through his short life John the Baptist was a man of the Word and the Spirit, for he lived in that reality as God's anointed man preparing for the Messiah.

Reflection

The song, 'These are the days of Elijah ...' may not be as popular today as it was in the past, but would to God, that more Elijah like prophetic figures appear among the churches in our nation. The first Elijah, and the second Elijah, John the Baptist, both spoke 'declaring the 'word of the Lord' and reading the texts about both it was often electrifying stuff. There was a directness about their preaching that is often lacking in today's pulpits, because there seems to be a view that the saints should never be disturbed – maybe tickled a bit, but not given the 'raw' word from above. I was fortunate to be live in the north (Scotland) and (Tyneside) where speaking truth meant speaking out. This often meant that there were times when the word spoken was sometimes 'blistering' and shook both heart and mind. It was humbling to hear men and women who spoke with an authority that is missing today. Two men stand out, one my namesake, Duncan Campbell known as the revivalist in the Hebrides Revivals. The occasion was a conference in Newcastle in the late 1960's – it was electrifying stuff with many under conviction - myself included. The other was James Philips of Edinburgh who was an outstanding biblical expositor who made the Scriptures come alive so that our hearts 'burned within us.' Both these men were men of the Word and Spirit and their Elijah like presence impacted the audiences. That kind of authority cannot be bought through attendance at theological seminaries – for their words were from above. Insipid preaching and teaching will do little for the people in the churches, and little for the people beyond the doors of the church. One of my friends, from the north again, managed to engage with working men in the town where he was a pastor and, to cut a long story short, he ended up simply expounding the Bible – the men and their families loved it because the Scriptures spoke the truth and some became disciples. Today, we do need those with pastoral hearts to preach with the authority that the Spirit gives which, over time, results in the transformation of cultures. Praying for Elijah's could be a cause 'celebre' – you've got to believe it!

The Spirit and the Conception of Jesus

Mary, a mid-teenage girl was engaged to Joseph, a righteous man, both enjoying their Jewish life – but their lives were about to change. On her part, the Jewish wedding was her focus, when she is suddenly confronted by angel Gabriel no less, one of God's constant messengers (Luke 1: 19, 26) who gives her his God-given message:

> 'Greetings, you who are highly favoured! The Lord is with you' (Luke 1: 28).

Teenagers, particularly girls, dream of many things, but angels! She must have been in a whirl! No wonder she was shaken, for why would an angel visit her at all? If it wasn't so serious, it's almost funny. Whatever Mary experienced then, and whatever she thought, little or nothing is said initially. Gabriel intervenes into Mary's thoughts and continues to share his message by offering her seven promises:

- The Lord is with you and you have found favour with God
- You will conceive in your womb and bear a son
- And you shall call his name Jesus
- He will be great, and will be called the Son of the Most High;
- And the Lord God will give to him the throne of his Father, David,
- And He will reign over the house of Jacob forever;
- And of his kingdom there will be no end (Luke 1: 31-33).

Mary immediately announces that she is a virgin, but undeterred Gabriel explains what is going to happen to her:

> 'The Holy Spirit will come upon you, and the Power of the Most High will overshadow you. So the holy one to be born will be called the Son of God' (Luke 1: 35).

Mary would have heard of the Spirit as a Jewish child, but would be fairly ignorant about how he works. Now she is to face becoming pregnant by the Spirit – even though she is a virgin. Her conception will be through the Spirit, not her on-coming husband. This was to be a miraculous action in her womb by the God who gives life – physically and spiritually. Whether this meant God would supply the sperm to go with Mary's egg is anyone's guess, but Mary would become pregnant. She overcame her shock, accepted the word of Gabriel and looked forward to the promise being fulfilled (Luke 1: 38). In the meantime, the two cousins meet up at Elizabeth's, who is also pregnant, and when Mary tells her she is pregnant, the baby in Elizabeth's womb 'leapt' within her, and Elizabeth was 'filed with the Holy Spirit' as she blessed God for the coming of the Messiah-child in Mary's womb.

The celebration continued, for Mary started to sing in the Spirit as she reflected on what this sudden change in her body actually meant for her and the nation of Israel, for she burst into song:

- My soul glorifies the Lord and my Spirit rejoices in God my Saviour
- The Lord knows me as a humble servant and generations will call me blessed
- The Mighty One has done great things for me – holy is his name
- His mercy extends from generation to generation
- He has performed mighty deeds – and scattered those who are proud
- He has brought down rulers and lifted up the humble
- He has filled the hungry with good things, but sent the rich away
- He has helped his servant Israel and has been merciful
- He has remembered our descendents and the promises made to Abraham

(Luke 1: 46-55)

Mary, continued her pregnancy until she reached full term, and through the Holy Spirit Jesus (Yeshuah) was born naturally. His conception was different because it was miraculous and supernatural. Joseph, chosen by God, was also spoken to by an angel (Gabriel again?), became Mary's husband and then the newborn King's stepfather. Salvation had arrived in the person of Jesus. The Spirit is linked immediately with new life and is a sign that the New Age had dawned. From his birth, Jesus was to become 'a man of the Spirit' for there was never a time when the Spirit was absent from his life. He lived constantly in the atmosphere of the Holy Spirit. These events contain so much and are a reminder that the work of the Holy Spirit was involved all the way through the coming of the Messiah – in the birth of Christ, the King of Kings.

Two further aspects need to be included here as part of the coming and arrival of Jesus:

Briefly there is the Christmas story itself in Matthew and Luke who tell us something of the event that took place around 4 BC. Matthew brings Joseph into the picture and there is the declaration:

> 'Mary ... will give birth to a son, and you are to give him the name Jesus, because he will save his people from their sins' for the 'virgin will conceive and give birth to a son, and they will call him Immanuel' (Matt. 1: 21, 23).

Luke's story centres on the town of Bethlehem where Mary gave birth and placed her child in a manger, for there was no guestroom available. The shepherds in the fields hear a great sound in the heavens as they are joined by an angelic host who sing:

> 'Glory to God in the highest heaven, and on earth peace to those on whom his favour rests' (Luke 2: 14).

> The family are soon joined by the wandering shepherds who, worshipping the child, 'returned, glorifying and praising God for all they had heard and seen ...' (Luke 2: 20).

The circumcision, purification and naming ceremony in the Temple, introduces us to two elderly saints. Simeon who was waiting for the 'consolation of Israel' – the coming of the Messiah – for the Holy Spirit had revealed to him 'that he would not die before he has seen the Lord's Messiah' (Luke 2: 26). Again, Simeon, now in the Temple courts is moved 'by the Spirit' and takes Jesus into his arms and prophesies over him:

- ➢ He praised God because the sovereign Lord had given what he promised
- ➢ His eyes have seen God's salvation for all nations
- ➢ A light of revelation has risen for the Gentiles
- ➢ The Messiah is the glory of Israel (Luke 2: 29-32).

Furthermore, Mary and Joseph are overwhelmed by the way Simeon blessed their chid, Jesus, for 'this child will be for the fall and rising of Israel. The thoughts of many hearts will be revealed through him and 'a sword will pierce' the heart of Mary (Luke 2: 33-36). Alongside

Simeon is Anna, a prophetess who, from widowhood has remained in the 'Temple for years, worshipping night and day, fasting and praying'(Luke 2: 36-38).

Two people believed the Messiah had come, for God had fulfilled his prophetic intentions.

The 'Song of Mary,' known today as the Magnificat or Canticle of Mary, (Luke 1: 46-55) was a wonderful meaningful prayer of thanksgiving. It is unlikely that Mary would have known a great deal of the phrases, some of which appear to be from the prophecy of Isaiah and the book of Psalms. True, she would have learned some of the phrases when attending the local synagogue, and she may have made up and sung songs of praise in her family home as a young person. Even then, there is no doubt that such a song message, is likely to have been given to her by the Holy Spirit for the words contain theological insights, related to the coming birth of her Son, Jesus – the Saviour of the world. Even so, what an amazing teenager she appears to have been, for she lived a 'righteous life' and was 'favoured by God,' so who else could have borne the Son of God, apart from this young woman?

To sum up, scene after scene in both Matthew and Luke, as they combine to alert us to the physical revelation of the coming of the Son of God, born to a virgin teenage girl, out of wedlock until she was married to Joseph. Throughout the different episodes of the story, with the prophetic promises, births, songs, the dominant activity of God as Father, Son and Holy Spirit is clearly demonstrated. There is much more to engage us in these events – than we realise – events that shook the world then and still do so. The Incarnation still puzzles the world of humanity today, and will continue to do that untill the end of time.

Reflection

The music of believers is different, unique and even holy for the intention is to engage in celebrating the Lord of Glory. There is no doubt that the songs that are part of the celebration around the Incarnation of Jesus are kingdom songs. They are heaven directed, due to the leading of the Spirit, and are spiritual, social and God directed. We regard Christian music as unique to those who sing, play and dance their faith. There is no indication that any of the people involved in the events around Jesus' birth, moved rhythmically, though it seems preposterous that the angelic choirs simply sang without movement – after all they were angels! Music, above all, is a servant of all God's people, a gift of grace, but when used in ministry takes on a servant role to the kingdom of God. Kingdom music is, first and foremost a lyric, using symbolic language and holistically brings life to Christian culture. The combined forces of voices and instruments aligned together, make the songs a breath of harmonious joy. There are probably three facets to Christian music:

- Kingdom music always has a message – a word that lives in the singers.
- Kingdom music has a purpose – for it endeavours to glorify God.
- Kingdom music is holistic and often healing.

John the Baptiser

In their opening sections, each of the four Gospels record the striking impact of Jesus' cousin, John the Baptist. Dressed like Elijah, he is the first prophet to appear in Israel for four hundred years. His camel-haired coat contrasted with the cultured religious leaders of the time. God speaks to the people through his prophet and urged them to change their way of life. His message was powerful and blunt: "Repent, for the kingdom of heaven in near" (Matt.3: 2). There was an immediacy about his preaching: 'It was now or never!' The time is short. The people must repent – they must turn away from their sins. The Day of the Lord is here. His words were about judgment, promise and forgiveness. They are called to confess their sins by submitting to being baptised in water in the river Jordan, as a symbol of their sins being washed away so they can receive the forgiveness of God. The kingdom of God is present, but more than that, the King is coming and will be with us:

"The axe is laid to the root of the trees and every tree that does not produce good fruit will be cut down and thrown into the fire. I baptise you with water for repentance. But after me will come one who is more powerful than I, the strap of whose sandals I am not worthy to stoop down and untie. I baptise you with water, but he will baptise you with the Holy Spirit and fire ... and will burn the chaff with unquenchable fire"(Matt. 3: 10-11).

Jesus arrives as John is baptising hundreds of people and, seen by the prophet, declares the profound purpose of Jesus' coming and presence: "Look, the Lamb of God, who takes away the sin of the world!" (John 1: 29). He has already exposed the Pharisees and Sadducees, the manipulative religious leaders from Jerusalem, by calling them a 'brood of vipers.' He demanded that they 'flee from God's wrath for they will be cut off' from the 'blessing of the future' unless they repent of their sins (Matt. 3: 8-9). With this tribute to Jesus as God's lamb, John was declaring that he was the Pascal Sacrificial Lamb of the Exodus, the story of Israel's redemption from the house of bondage (Ex. 12: 1-11). Jesus is portrayed as the one and only person who is the 'redeemer-King' through whom reconciliation can be granted. John's unveiling or revelation of Jesus is, for him, a confirmation of his role as the 'forerunner' and 'herald' of the Messiah-King chosen by God. (John 1: 6; 31).

Reflection

Being a spokesperson for God is never an easy calling. You only have to read the stories of the prophets in the Old Testament. The same is true of the disciples in the New Testament. Legend has it that the original apostles lost their lives through the activity of the forces of darkness. The apostle John did survive, but lived out the later part of his life in an island prison on Patmos (Rev. 1: 9). The history of the Early Church records period after period when the Christians and Church's were put to the sword, but by the fourth century AD the Christian faith became the main religious faith in the Roman Empire. The persecution of Christians has resulted in hundreds of thousands losing freedom by being imprisoned, or their losing their lives at the behest of secular governments, other religions and paganism. Despite that, despite the persecution, the calling of God to 'go and speak' is so written in the hearts of many believers, that sharing faith is a constant for them. It is a well known fact that the assault on Christians is at an all time high across the world today. Despite that, the church is still growing and impacting the cultures they serve, especially in the continents of Africa, Asia, and the Middle East. True, much of Western Europe is something of a disaster area when it comes to the Gospel, but Eastern Europe has seen some amazing signs of spiritual church growth in the last thirty years. There is a modern 'shout' for the church in the UK to re-evangelise the nation, but that will take faith, courage and determination throw aside our 'comfort jackets' and engage the enemy. For too long churches have been long on talk, but short on evangelistic action, but there does appear to be a shift in the hearts of numbers of congregations that have started to engage with their local communities. The calling is to catch the 'fire' and stir up God's gift and follow suit (2 Cor. 5: 14-15; 20-21) – be ambassadors for Christ.

The Jordan River

John had been baptising people in the river Jordan near the town of Bethany, and was astonished when Jesus stepped into the waters, demanding that he be baptised by the prophet. The irascible preacher tried to avoid baptising his cousin, but Jesus prevailed, and there, before the crowds, he was baptised by immersion for Jesus came 'up out of the water' (Mark 1: 10). What John did with others, he did with Jesus. Jesus was not baptised for his sin, because he was without sin – he was baptised to identify with sinful humankind – past, present and future (Heb. 4: 15). His 'water baptism' was not a metaphor for Spirit baptism, as one scholar remarked, but a baptism of righteousness as he identified with lost people. In a word, Jesus was saying there is another way – the way of faith – the way of fresh beginnings. Later, prior to his ascension, Jesus insisted that baptism was a marker for true disciples for he insisted that the apostolic team were to baptise those who professed faith in Christ(Matt. 28: 18-20). The implications of his baptism were profound for him, as witnessed in heaven and on earth, and for future generations of his followers in every age.

The facts of his baptism are clear from the witnesses who were present. Jesus is in the water with John and he is praying – praying to his Father (Luke 3: 21). It was as he was praying 'heaven opened' or was 'torn open' for the Greek word used here is the same word used of the 'curtain of the temple which was torn in two, from top to bottom' Mark 3; 10; Matt. 27: 11) and the 'splitting of the stones when Jesus died' Matt. 27: 51). The whole of heaven was ripped apart to allow the Father to 'see' his Son being baptised. In all probability the cosmos, the archangels and the angelic host were heavenly witnesses to the scene in the river Jordan. This was a moment for heaven and earth to celebrate Jesus' baptism. The link between Jesus' baptism and his death show clearly that Jesus was anointed for sacrifice, as well as empowerment for service. All four Gospels tell us that the Spirit of God came down on Jesus from on high – from the throne of God – accompanied by a dove while still in the water. The physical action of the dove could be a reference to the 'dove' sent out by Noah which eventually returned to the ark, as a symbol of the start of a New Age (Gen.8:10). Thus the arrival of Jesus was the start of the New Age of the kingdom. In the water Jesus was drenched in the Holy Spirit even though he had the Spirit, this overwhelming at his baptism was to enable him to fulfil his Father's plan, to glorify him and transform the lives of people. Immediately this happened, "a voice from heaven is heard" by the witnesses, "You are my Son whom I love; with you I am well pleased" (Luke 3: 22). This personal intimate loving moment between Father and Son, that his baptism was a global display to the world, the cosmos, and to the powers of darkness, that Jesus was being set apart for ministry. From that moment Jesus became conscious of a new authority and charismatic power to forgive sinners, heal the sick, raise the dead and to teach and preach the kingdom of God. The graphic picks out the events of his baptism in water and the Spirit:

A Voice from Heaven

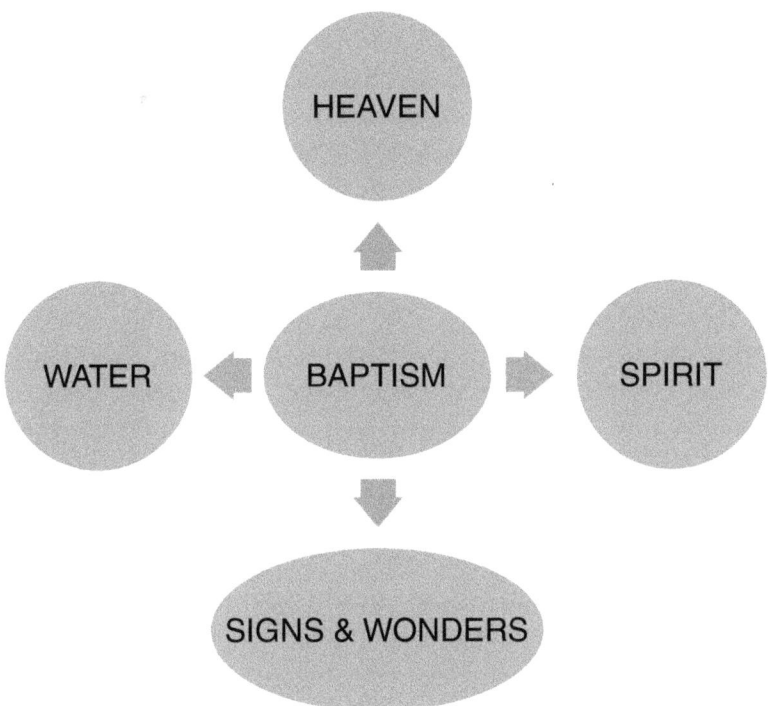

The Adversary

According to Luke, the Holy Spirit was at work in Jesus' conception, so during his early years and before he became an adult, he was a person of the Spirit. His high calling is acknowledged by the angel Gabriel, who announced prophetically that he will 'reign over' the house of David and Jacob 'forever; his kingdom will never end' (Luke 1; 32-33).

Mark Tells us that Jesus was 'sent' or 'driven' by the Spirit to engage with Satan in the desert or wilderness (Mark 1: 13). The forceful direction through the Spirit brought Jesus face to face with the forces of darkness and evil, in the person of Satan. This open conflict between the Messianic-King and his adversary is a signal for both Jesus and his followers that such battles will be common place. Jesus spent forty days and nights fasting (Matt. 4: 2), it was only after enjoying time with his Father that the enemy began to tempt him. The temptations Jesus faced were given to test out whether he would abandon his call to be the Messiah, avoid preaching the kingdom of God, and put aside the offer of salvation through his death on the cross. Each temptation was repeated again and again, rather than on just three separate occasions, and tuned to undermine the purpose of his coming. Being baptised in water and the Spirit was a special moment, but suddenly his intellect, emotions, will, spirit, physical and mental strength is being attacked.

> It was a repeat attack: 'If,' 'If,' 'If,' you are the Son of God, make these stones bread, throw yourself from the Temple precincts, accept the kingdoms of this world – such was the battering he received (Luke 4: 4-13). Jesus overcame every temptation by using the 'sword of the Spirit ... the Word of God' (Eph. 6: 17): 'It is written ... It is written ... It is written' (Deut. 8: 3; 6: 13, 16).

Jesus knew his Torah, his Bible, and by that Word and through the Spirit, responded to Satan's subtle words. Jesus, exhausted after this onslaught, came out the stronger and was ministered to by angels. After all, Jesus' kingdom is eternal, Satan's kingdom is temporal. There can be no compromise with darkness. Jesus refused to be drawn away from his purpose and rejected his adversaries' overtures. The four Gospels contain excerpts of the way Jesus continued to encounter various onslaughts from the enemy of souls. Satan sent out his 'attack dogs' in the form of the Pharisees, Sadducees, Scribes and Elders – to undermine his teaching, mock his ministry of healing, accuse him of blasphemy, attribute his gifts to Beelzebub and set out to have him murdered – before Calvary (Mark 2: 18-3; 3: 20-30; 11: 27-33). Jesus faced the persecution and trial, sustained by God the Spirit and

> "... returned to Galilee in the power of the Spirit, and news about him spread through the whole countryside. He taught in their synagogues, and everyone praised him" (Like 4:14-15).

Reflection

The film, *Jesus of Nazareth*, on general release many years ago, followed the Synoptic Gospel's fairly accurately, probably because they used the KJV text, and yes, they did use quotations from that translation. One of the key elements in the film, but missed by many filmgoers, was a shadowy figure that appeared at important parts of the film. In virtually every key scene, if you watched carefully the shadow of a person could be spotted hovering near Jesus. The shadow represented Satan and in scene after scene, if you watched the film with genuine interest you would become aware of the influences of evil and darkness as Jesus speaks and heals. Whoever came up with that idea as part of the film script – though the shadow never said anything – must have read the Gospel storey comprehensively. Interestingly, in the last scene, the shadow is by the cross on which Jesus died, but when it comes to the scene of the resurrection there is no shadow!

In the days after his baptism and anointing in the river Jordan, Jesus attended his home town synagogue in Nazareth, where he was invited to read from the Tenakh (the Hebrew Bible), and was handed, the set passage of Isaiah 61: 1-2 which confirms his calling as Messiah: "The Spirit of the Lord is on me, because the Lord has anointed me to preach the good news to the poor ... "(Luke 4: 16-18). Other passages would probably have come to the mind of Jesus as he stood before the congregation on that Shabbat day:

"And he will be called Wonderful Counsellor, Mighty God, Everlasting Father, Prince of Peace. Of his government and peace there will be no end" (Isa. 9: 6-7).

"The Spirit of wisdom will rest on him – the Spirit of wisdom and of understanding, the Spirit of counsel and of power, the Spirit of knowledge and of the fear of the Lord – and he will delight in the fear of the Lord" (Isa. 11: 2-3).

"He was pierced for our transgressions, he was crushed for our iniquities; the punishment that brought us peace was upon him, and by his wounds we are healed" (Isa. 53: 5).

The inauguration of Jesus' calling is clear in the prophecies, and is mentioned by the apostle Peter when preaching in the house of Cornelius some fifteen years later:

"You know what has happened throughout Judea, beginning at Galilee after the baptism that John preached – how God anointed Jesus of Nazareth with the Holy Spirit and power, and how he went about doing good things and healing all who were under the devil, because God was with him" (Acts 10: 37-38).

Clothed with power from the Spirit, Jesus was able to demonstrate the dynamic reign of God on earth. Within days he began preaching, teaching and healing for the blind could see, the deaf hear, the dumb speak, lepers were cured, evil spirits cast out and the dead raised (Mark 1: 21-2: 12; 7: 24-37; 8: 22-26; Matt. 9: 18-26)).

The Implications

The baptisms of Jesus – water and the Spirit – raise a number of insights that offer ways to the readers of the Gospels, to recognise the implications of Jesus' experience:

Jesus' baptism in the Jordan replicates the wilderness crossing into the Promised Land (Deut. 34: 4). Some archaeologists have suggested that the place where Jesus was baptised, near Bethany, was the same place where Joshua crossed the river Jordan to enter Canaan. The scene is pictured in Joshua chapters 3-4. After the people's consecration before the Lord, the Ark of the Covenant was carried by the priests, who stood together in the river – the river stops flowing and they cross to the other side. Jesus would have known the story from boyhood and perhaps it was a reminder that he would be involved in battles after his baptism in the Jordan, and empowerment in the Spirit. Christian's would do well to remember that from day one – the day we become disciples, that day we enter to an ongoing battlefield, but with Jesus we can win through in his strength.

The fact that the Spirit descended like a dove on Jesus, is a reminder that the Spirit can be sensitive and can be grieved by insensitive believers. Doves are prone to rest where it is peaceful and will depart when there is noise or disturbance. We have a dove that sits on our chimney daily and remains there sometimes indefinitely, but when there is any unexpected noise will soon fly away, and return when the noise is gone. If we reflect on the fact that the Spirit is like the Dove – and is highly sensitive - perhaps some of our frenetic relationships might improve!

> Jesus baptism in water and in the Spirit is a model for believers. He did no teaching, healing and miracles prior to his baptism. In other words, Jesus did not have the Father's authority as a man to act supernaturally until he was baptised in the waters of the Jordan, nor did he have the ability to fulfil his ministry to the people until he was baptised in the Spirit. Yes, Jesus was unique – he was God in human flesh (John 1: 14) – but could do no 'mighty works until clothed from above.' Therefore, Jesus as the Son of God, needed the Spirit to do the' mighty works' so how much more should Christian's covet the baptism in the Spirit – a drenching in the Spirit to preach the gospel of the kingdom of God with signs following?

The word 'Trinity' does not appear anywhere in the Bible. Nevertheless, the word is introduced here because it conveys deep spiritual and theological truths. Throughout the Bible God is presented as the Father, the Son and the Spirit – three-in-one.' Each person of the Trinity is of the same essence which conveys to us the richness of the Godhead. In the baptism of Jesus, the Father 'speaks,' the Son 'submits,' and the Spirit 'sends.' Each member of the Trinity was totally involved in Jesus' baptism. This is the divine family working together for one purpose - to glorify Jesus, God's only Son and advance the kingdom of God. This really calls on believers to offer a 'berakah' – a thanksgiving - to the Father, Son and Holy Spirit.

The Spirit in the Ministry of Jesus

Jesus, having been baptised in water and the Spirit, began his ministry in Galilee, his home territory. He knew, right from the start, that he only had so many years to fulfil his Father's plan. In a word, Jesus was in a hurry – he wanted to get the job done – and if you read the Gospel's carefully you will find that he determined to teach, preach and heal – as he moved around the nation. Mark, the supposed author of the Gospel, had grasped that and if you read the KJV translation his writing is full of activity. In other words there was an immediacy about Jesus, for he had a strategic purpose to proclaim the message of the kingdom of God to Jews, Gentiles and Samaritans. No sooner had Jesus referred to the fact that the kingdom was now present, that the New Age had begun, he then became an evangelist! Yes, the Messiah-King, the Son of Man and the Son of God was on a mission. There was a fire burning within heart and mind, and the time was short, so he started with his home area in the synagogues on Shabbat in Capernaum and Nazareth (Mark 1: 15, 21-28; Luke 4: 18-19,31-36). In both towns, he taught the Scriptures (the Tenack) with such authority, the people were amazed for he made the Scriptures live. In both towns, two men who had impure spirits were completely healed just by a word of command. Both communities were in uproar, for something remarkable had taken place in both towns, the men were healed for the evil spirits were cast out – the men were transformed. What a start to Jesus' mission, but there was also opposition from men who took umbrage, for it was the wrong day, and who was this man anyway? The God-Man Jesus, now fully anointed by the Spirit, had come from heaven to spread the good news, call nations back to God, and build a new community that would ultimately live forever!

> The Spirit Anoints Jesus to preach the Gospel (Matt.3:16-17; Mark 1:10,12; Luke 4:15-18)

After Jesus' anointing by the Spirit in the river Jordan, he 'returned in the power of the Spirit into Galilee, and a report concerning him went out throughout all the surrounding country. As he taught in their synagogues

> "The Spirit of the Lord is upon me, because he has anointed me to preach the good news ... "(Luke 4: 15-18).

We need to remind ourselves that what happened in the river Jordan was confirmation that Jesus was the Messiah, for the Father confirmed to John the Baptist when he 'sees the Spirit come down and remain' that Jesus was Messiah (John 1: 33). The question is, how does John 'see' the Spirit, and what were the evidences that the apostle knew that Jesus was truly the Messiah. Some have argued that it was the dove – but there is really more here and that is, that something happened to Jesus – to his person, for he was overwhelmed by the Spirit – he was drenched in the gift sent by the Father's favour. This was an extraordinary event because for 400 years (from Malachi to AD 26?) the Holy Spirit had been invisible in Israel. In addition to that reality, the coming of the Spirit from then on, meant that he would remain until the End of the Age. In the meantime, until that happened, that Age of the Spirit would continue. One other factor, is that Jesus himself would immerse people in the Holy Spirit (Pentecost) – and drench them in the personal empowering presence of the Father (Mark 1: 10). When Jesus stood to read the Hebrew scroll from the book of Isaiah (61: 1-2), he was declaring his mandate as prophet, priest and king – the Messiah had come! He was so full of the Spirit that his teaching caused commotion among the people, for he insisted that his mission was to the marginalised – the poor, the captives, the blind, the prisoners of bondage and oppression, which turned out to be anathema to the audience (Luke 4: 20-.24). Then to cap it all, he referred back to Elijah's ministry to two Gentiles, the widow of Zarephath, and Naaman a leper, without mentioning the prophet's ministry to the Jews, causing consternation. In their fury they threw Jesus out of the synagogue, took him to the brow of the hill to throw him off the cliff – only for Jesus to walk through the angry crowd (Luke 4:22-30). In announcing his salvation message of the good news of the kingdom of God, he was stating that a New Age had arrived. Some commentators have played down his Spirit baptism in the Jordan, by insisting it was his divine nature that enabled him to carry out his mandate. To play down his anointing undermines his humanity, for as Son of Man, his ministry was for the oppressed.

The Spirit and Spiritual Darkness (Mark 5: 15; Luke 8: 30; Matt. 12: 28; 26: 53)

Reading the gospel accounts of Jesus ministry among the people is something of a revelation, because it is apparent that the authorities are constantly biting at Jesus' heals! His work (Gk: erga) among the people was dogged by the religious authorities who were, to all intents and purposes, working for another kingdom – the kingdom of darkness. Jesus was in a synagogue on Shabbat when his enemies set a trap by pointing out a man with a shrivelled hand, so Jesus healed him – but it was the wrong day! The antagonists were not interested in the man, but in using the man to undermine Jesus' authority. Jesus carried on healing the people that followed him, while Matthew adds a footnote from Isaiah the prophet:

> "Here is my servant whom I have chosen, the one I love, in whom I delight; I will put my Spirit on him, and he will proclaim justice to the nations ... in his Name nations will put their trust" (Isa. 42: 1-4).

In the middle of constant antagonism, Jesus healed a man who was demon-possessed, blind and mute. Once Jesus exorcised the man, he immediately began to see and speak, which astonished the crowd who voiced out loud, 'Could this be the Son of David' (Matt. 12: 22-23). The Pharisees, hearing this, reacted with fury and responded by accusing Jesus of healing the man through Beelzebub, the prince of demons (Matt. 12: 24). Jesus for his part makes a categorical announcement:

> "If it is by the Spirit of God that I cast out demons, then the kingdom of God has come upon you" (Matt. 12: 28).

Jesus' healing ministry was ongoing, and miraculous moments were happening to people time and again, but this particular healing was a dramatic demonstration and declaration that Jesus, under the authority of the Holy Spirit, was appointed to heal. His authority comes from who he is – the Son of Man. The sin of the Pharisees is that they attribute to Satan what Jesus, the Son of God, has done and in doing so blasphemed against the Holy Spirit. Such a sin will never be forgotten or forgiven in this age or in the age to come (Matt. 12: 31-32; Mark 3:29). In our contemporary world there are those who believe they are able to cast out evil spirits who happen to be psychic healers or belong to New Age teams (still active), but much of what they say is unreliable and fantasy. Believers, who have the same Holy Spirit as Jesus, are sometimes involved in acts of exorcism, but this should be done with great care and by leaders who are skilled in this ministry. To be engaged in such a ministry demands that the people involved are fully aware of the challenges, for much prayer and dependence upon the Holy Spirit is required, for he is the one who acts in Jesus' name.

The Spirit of Joy and Prayer (Luke 10: 9,17,18, 21; 11: 13)

> "At that time Jesus, full of joy in the Holy Spirit, said: I praise you Father, Lord of heaven and earth, because you have hidden these things from the wise and the learned, and revealed them to little children. Yes, Father for this was your good pleasure" (Luke 10: 21).

The context is the mission of the 70 or 72 who were commissioned by Jesus, to go in 'two's' to 'heal the sick' and 'tell them the kingdom of God is near …' (Luke10: 9). Later, they returned 'with joy and said, 'Lord even the demons submit to us in your name' (Luke 10: 1, 9,17). The description of Jesus being overcome with joy in the Holy Spirit (Gk: en to pneumatic), indicates that Jesus simply celebrates 'in the Spirit' for the way the disciples saw people transformed, and for the fact that the powers of darkness were damaged as 'Satan fell from Heaven' (Luke 10: 18). The men, probably trembling at the challenge given to them, were able to return to Jesus full of pleasure at the submission of evil spirits to the 'name of Jesus' (Luke 10: 17). In keeping with the tension between the righteous and wicked, Jesus warned them to celebrate that their 'names are written in heaven' rather than mocking their opponents with victory over the demons (Luke 10: 20).

Jesus' 'joy in the Spirit' enables him to worship his Father who is Lord of the cosmos, but wisely hides 'gospel truths' from the religious establishment – the wise and the learned – but unveils the 'hidden things' to little children (Luke 10: 21). The 'little children' may refer literally to small children or could stand as a metaphor for childlike trust that opens the door into the kingdom of God (Matt. 18; 1-4)

The Promise of the Father (Luke 11: 13; Acts 1: 4)

One of the most well know passages in the Gospels, is the Lucan rendering of the Lord's Prayer, at which point Jesus, insists they learn to pray similarly to: "Father, hallowed by your name, your kingdom come, may your will be done on earth as it is in heaven … " (11: 2; Matt. 6: 9-13). This is followed by a parable story of a friend who keeps knocking on the door for some bread, the householder is initially annoyed, but decides to give the man what he needs. It was the constant banging on the door for some bread that caused the owner of the house to act. Jesus was giving the disciples an example of importunate, pleading prayer – ask, seek, knock – and everyone who does that will be blessed by God (Luke 11:9-10). To re-enforce the discipline of such prayer he engages in teasing the disciples about giving gifts to their children they don't want, for most families even if evil, will still offer good gifts to their children. Jesus then moves into talking about the goodness of the Father in heaven who will 'give the Holy Spirit to those who ask him' (Luke 11: 13). The Holy Spirit is a gift – the best gift – the gift believers need to enable them to fully engage in charismatic ministry. He is referring here to the Pentecostal gift that each disciple can enjoy, and is anticipating the time when the disciples await the coming of the Spirit in the Upper Room in Jerusalem (Acts 1: 4-5, 8) which the disciples did. They waited for the promise of the Father constantly praying for ten days for the coming of the Spirit, until "the Spirit came upon them" (Acts 2: 1). Jesus is not referring to the inner work of the Spirit here – he is not talking about regeneration but empowerment for 'you shall receive power' (Acts 1: 8) is the key phrase. In other words being empowered would enable believers to proclaim God's kingdom, heal the sick, contend with evil and spiritual darkness. Yes, they did that before Pentecost because Jesus gave them special authority to do that (Luke 9: 1-6). The problem was that Jesus was also preparing to leave them after the cross and the resurrection, and because he was not with them physically, he could not give them that authority. Pentecost changed all that, for on that day the 120 disciples were baptised in the Spirit, and the power of God fell on them enabling them to act as Jesus had done when with them. The Spirit, who is another of the same, now replaced Jesus, meaning he could now work though his people wherever they were (John 14: 16-17). Today, the same Father, through the Son, will give the Holy Spirit of power to those who ask him(Luke 11: 13).

Reflection

While on a renewal mission near Baltimore, in the United States, we held a prayer ministry time on a Monday evening in a church hall. We had spent a week working with the church preaching, teaching and building kingdom relationships. We were a group of 20 people from a London church, with two teams. The church we were with had around 300 members, and opened their hearts to us, but gave us the freedom to establish ongoing friendships. The meeting was our last planned time, because we were due to leave the next day. Over twenty-five people came to the fellowship time together. We read the Scriptures, prayed, worshipped together and waited on the Spirit. This was a very dignified and open-hearted time and we sensed the presence of the Spirit among us. One person, a young army officer, was to leave that week to fly to a troublesome post in the Middle East. He began to gently shake as he stood with us. Within minutes he was sitting in a chair worshipping the Lord silently. Others began to experience the same as the Spirit moved among us. We sensed the time was right to hold hands and be open to what the Lord wanted to say to us. We sensed a spirit of love descending upon us, and by this time most were standing, some lost in God, while others were praying quietly in tongues. There was a real anointing of the Spirit in the meeting which some confessed to being entirely new for them in their spiritual journey. At the end of the evening I shared some time with the Army Captain who, knowing he was going to a volatile area had been fearful about his posting. The 'fear' had gone and in its place was a new sense of God's peace and joy, with a new language – having never spoken in tongues – he was now confident he would be able to lead his men physically, emotionally and spiritually. It was an evening of meaning for all of us, but especially for the number who were baptised in the Spirit   The friendships made, and the time spent spiritually enriched the Team and the local Church of God, and finished with songs of praise to the Lord of glory.

The Spirit and Jesus (John 1: 32-33, 34; 3: 34; 4: 23-24; 7: 38-39)

John the Baptist bears witness to the experience of Jesus after his water baptism, for he said:

> "I saw the Spirit come down from heaven as a dove and remain on him ... who will baptise with the Holy Spirit ... I have seen and testify that he is the Son of God. For the one whom God has sent speaks the words of God, for God gives the Spirit without limit" (John 1: 32-33).

John's account matches the records of Jesus' baptism in the Gospels. The word about the Spirit remaining on Jesus is used twice in the narrative. On the first occasion the verb 'remaining' is in the aorist tense (Gk: emeinen), while on the second occasion a present participle 'remaining' (Gk: menon) is used, indicating a permanent on-going relationship. This relationship with the Spirit is a vital element in Jesus' effective ministry for he is in such intimacy with the Spirit, that everything he says and does – words and the works – carry the authority of the Son through the Spirit. After all, Jesus himself, at the Father's appointed time, will baptise believers with the Holy Spirit from the Day of Pentecost onwards. He will do so from his exalted position at the right hand of the Father (Acts 1: 8; Eph.4: 7-8).

There is a hint of the coming charismatic Pentecost when Jesus shouted to the crowds with a loud voice during the Feast of Tabernacles, and declared:

> "If anyone is thirsty, let him come to me and drink. Whoever believes in me, as the Scripture has said, streams of living water will flow from within him. By this he meant the Spirit, whom those who believed in him were later to receive. Up to that time the Spirit had not been given, since Jesus had not been glorified" (John 7: 37-39).

Being thirsty is the criteria – a longing for the blessing of a fuller life – but the thirst here is different from the thirst Jesus spoke about to the adulterous woman (John 4: 13). The 'spring of water' he was referring to, was the well of 'eternal life' – the new birth. His intention here in John 7 is different for he is looking forward to a future event. This event will only come after Jesus is glorified on Calvary's cross, and after his resurrection from the borrowed Tomb. It was then, and only then, according to John's Gospel, that Jesus was glorified. There is no doubt that Jesus himself is the one who contains the 'streams of living water' but it is also clear that the thirsty can drink from the well of blessing through Christ himself, by the Spirit. For Pentecost is the means by which believers are baptised in the Spirit, which in terms of the metaphor of the 'living water, is to enjoy personally the same as being baptised in the Holy Spirit. Jesus does not link 'the streams of living water' here to the work of regeneration, but to the streams of water bubbling up from within, due to being drenched by Jesus, the Baptiser of the Spirit. Baptism in the Spirit has an effect on the whole person – the will, the mind, the emotions – it is an overwhelming conscious experience when a person is drenched in God, by the Spirit. When this experience does happen – people are not passive – for they know something has happened to them. It is known and felt and witnessed by other people if present, who know something dynamic has happened to that person. It is a baptism of power, the power of the Spirit, with which to carry out serving Christ the King in the theatre of the world of broken people. It is this that Christians today are urged to seek – a personal empowerment by the Spirit, an emphasis that is underlined in different sections of this study.

The Spirit and Salvation (John 1: 12; 3: 1-18; 6: 63; 14: 6; 20: 31)

"... to those who believed in his name, he gave the right to become the children of God" (John 1:12). People often make the mistake of believing that every person on planet earth is automatically a child of God – wrong! We are not born as God's children for we are not God's children by nature. We only become children of God when we believe in Jesus as Lord and Saviour and that it is the Spirit of God that brings that about, and confirms that we are children of God by God's choice (John 15: 16). Jesus, in conversation with Nicodemus, insists in reply to the Pharisee evasive remarks:

> 'I tell you the truth, no one can enter the kingdom of God unless he is born of water and the Spirit. Flesh gives birth to flesh, but the Spirit gives birth to the Spirit ... the wind blows wherever it pleases, you hear its sound, but you cannot tell where it comes from or where it is going. So it is with everyone born of the Spirit" (John 3: 5-8).

Later, on another occasion, Jesus specifies the difference between the flesh and the Spirit: "It is the Spirit that gives life, the flesh is of no avail; the words I have spoken to you are Spirit and life" (John 6: 63). The very words of God – the teachings of the Scriptures by Jesus, other teachers and the prophets, are full of the life – 'the life of God in the soul of man' (Scougal). This means that the very Word of God - the Bible – are not just words, they are God's words through the Spirit (2 Tim. 3: 16). Returning to the Nicodemus story, the Pharisee and 'university teacher' was dumfounded by Jesus, even more so when he insisted that:

> "God so loved the world that he gave his only Son, that whoever believes in him should not perish but have eternal life. For God did not send his Son into the world to condemn the world, but to save the world through him" (John 16-17).

Yes, I know some scholars regard John chapter 3: 16-21, as additions by another writer, perhaps the apostle himself, or one of the disciples. But the arguments for this are somewhat flimsy for this discussion between the two Rabbi's' must have gone on for hours, so I will stick with the traditional view. The reference to the Spirit here is mainly about the work of regeneration, though Jesus does stress the freedoms the Holy Spirit has in other areas beyond regeneration.

When Jesus talked with his disciples during his final Passover Week, he anticipated leaving them in a few days, and spoke carefully about 'mansions' in glory that were for his followers. The disciples, still confused, left it to Thomas to ask the question: "'... we don't know where you are going, so how can we know the way" (John 14: 5). In reply, Jesus defined who he was, yet again, but this time put it across in another skilled retort: "I am the way and the truth and the life. No one comes to the Father except through me" (John 14: 6). Thus for them, as for others, salvation is only through Jesus, the Son of God, for he is the way to God, the truth about God, and the life of God. Simple, but powerful, which led to further conversations with other disciples. Jesus was obviously determined, during his last week with them to offer something beyond what they had experienced – a place in glory – but at the same time to assure them that they would be strengthened by what they believed, and by the gift of the Counsellor (John 14: 16) which we will consider after this section. But first, it is worth noting that the Gospel of John had a specific purpose when written:

> "Jesus did many other miraculous signs in the presence of the disciples, which are not recorded in this book. But these are written that you may believe that Jesus is the Christ, the Son of God, and that by believing you may have life in his name" (John 20: 30-31).

This 'eternal life' that Jesus referred to in his conversation with Nicodemus, was the very life of Christ himself through the Spirit, that the Pharisee would only understand after Jesus' death on Calvary and his resurrection from the tomb. There is every likelyhood that Nicodemus did become a follower of Jesus for he, with Joseph of Arimathea were involved in Jesus' burial (John 19: 38-42).

The Spirit as Counsellor (John 14: 16-17; 26, 15: 25-26; 16: 7-8, 13, 15)

> "And I will ask the Father, and he will give you another Counsellor to be with you forever – the Spirit of truth. The world cannot accept him, because it nether sees him, nor knows him. For he lives with you and will be in you" John 14: 15-17).

It is the night before Jesus' death and Jesus starts to speak to the disciples about the Holy Spirit. He offers to speak to his Father on their behalf so that his Father will give them another Counsellor (Gk: parakletos) which means one who stands alongside them. The Greek word was used in a Roman court of Law as a means of support, encouragement, counsel and be their personal advocate. To talk about 'another Counsellor' means literally 'another of the same' someone like Jesus who had been with the disciples for over three years. The only difference is that the Counsellor is not visible, but he is personal not impersonal, and will be with them all the time. He will be with them permanently – forever! He is all powerful, just like the other members of the Godhead – the Father and the Son. The key to enjoying the blessings of the parakletos is to love Jesus, and in loving Jesus they will enjoy the Father's love (John 14: 21), for the 'Father himself loves you' (John 16: 27).

> "The Counsellor, the Holy Spirit, whom the Father will send in my name, will teach you all things and will remind you of everything I have said to you" (John 14:26).

If the disciples were worried about recalling all that Jesus taught them, the Spirit will refresh their mind about what they learned – the Spirit becomes the teacher. "When he, the Spirit of truth comes, he will guide you into all truth." Importantly, the Holy Spirit teaches believers all things, including the way to live in obedience to Christ. This is the kind of work the Holy Spirit specializes in when directing believers in their journey.

"When he (the Holy Spirit) comes, he will convict the world of guilt in regard to sin and righteousness and judgment. In regard to sin, because men do not believe in me, in regard to righteousness, because I am going to the Father, ... and in regard to judgment because the prince of this world now stands condemned" (John 16: 8-12).

One factor, which preachers are aware of, is that it is the Holy Spirit who makes the Scriptures live so it should be quite common for people to be 'under conviction of sin' in a Christian meeting. This does not mean that the person makes the confession of their sin – that may come – but in many respects the person may just be uncomfortable but may not be sure why. This might go on for weeks until some help is sought.

Reflection

One of my friends who was resident in Edinburgh when studying at University, would regularly attend a Kirk (Church of Scotland) where a well-known preacher was the Pastor. He did so, he told me, because time and again through the exposition of Scripture he would come away under conviction. Now, he was a believer then, but for him it was a means of 'testing out' his relationship with the Lord. This was certainly unusual, but why should believers not 'feel' the impact of the Word on them, and reform their behaviour. In a word, is that not what preaching is for – for the Body of Christ. Yes, sadly, for many in the pews the teaching – if there is teaching – is so lacking in power and authority that many leave without ever being really impacted by the Word of God. By and large, when the Spirit is present and the Word is taught, he will convict 'the world of humankind of sin, guilt, unrighteousness and eventual judgment.' It may appear that the un-churched get off scot free, because the world in which they live is outside the boundaries of the Christian faith – but the truth is opposite, for God never leaves himself without a witness because his Spirit works across humankind whether they are kingdom people or not! The Father 'does not want "anyone to perish, but everyone to come to repentance" (2 Pet. 3: 9). Jesus and the Spirit work together, for the Holy Spirit represents Jesus to the people. To clarify the ministries of both Jesus and the Spirit, Jesus functions in heaven on behalf of believers, while the Spirit functions on earth to support believers through life's adventures. Comprehensively, both members of the Trinity, along with the Father, care for God's people whether in heaven or on earth. What an amazing, creative, loving, generous, faithful God we have, who always has our best interests at heart.

The Spirit, the Mission and the Church (John 20; 21-23)

> "Peace be with you!" said Jesus, "As the Father has sent me, I am sending you." And with that he breathed on them and said, "Receive the Holy Spirit. If you forgive anyone sins, they are forgiven: if you do not forgive them, they are not forgiven" (John 20: 21-23).

The disciples were in their favourite house is Jerusalem – a house that had many memories – and as they were pondering what had already happened that day with some appearances of Jesus on the 1st day of the week, Sunday. Jesus then appeared to them visibly in the 'Upper Room' and greeted them with 'peace' (Gk: eirene) or if Hebrew 'shalom', meaning 'life made whole' because Jesus was back with his loved ones – his disciples. Jesus is the Son who is the 'sent one' by and from the Father with a mission proclaiming the Father's love. His mandate was to become their mandate for they are to 'go out into the world' with the gospel message of the kingdom of God: "As the Father sent me, I am sending you"(cf. Matt. 28: 18-20). To encourage them to act out their commission he 'breathes on them' (Gk: emphysao) and said, 'Receive the Holy Spirit.' The breathing or blowing on them echoes the act of God breathing life into Adam (Gen. 2: 7) and life into the dry bones in Ezekiel's vision (37: 14). The word 'receive' (Gk: aorist) is a present imperative which never has a future meaning, thereby as they received the Holy Spirit, they were given authority to forgive sins and/or withhold forgiveness as they shared the gospel. Let's endeavour to unpack what is happening in the Upper Room with Jesus:

Jesus is calling the apostolic team to be as he was for as the Father sent him, so he is sending the disciples on a global mission: 'As the Father sent me, so I am sending you' so they are given the same authority. This recalls their first venture into mission as recorded by Matthew:

> "He (Jesus), called the twelve disciples to him and gave them authority to drive out evil spirits and to heal every disease and sickness" (10: 1).

The 'authority' he gave then, is the same authority he is imparting to them now (20: 22), the only difference being that it is the resurrected Christ who is commissioning the team. Some have argued that the 'giving of the Holy Spirit' in the Upper Room was prophetic, or a parable, or symbol for the disciples relating to Pentecost. Such views appear to be somewhat arbitrary – and don't fit the context. All three of those suggestions are suspect, for what is taking place is that the disciples are being prepared for mission and are given an anointing to carry out what they were called to do. This is not related to Pentecost, for the Festival is still fifty days away! Literally, Jesus gave the disciples a specific experience of the Spirit when he said, 'receive the Spirit' after 'breathing' on them. The physical act was a metaphor linked to the Spirit being received. This is not about the coming Pentecost for the word 'receive' is in the present tense and is about a specific experience of the Spirit related to a) the offer of forgiveness or b) the preparatory times prior to Pentecost – for support during the 40 days and/or the 10 days of importunate prayer.

> Something else is happening in the Upper Room, which is sensitive and vibrant and it relates to the disciples being given the right to offer forgiveness. There could be a link here with Jesus announcement of building "my church and the gates of hell shall not prevail against it" (Matt. 16: 18 ESV). Having committed the disciples to a triumphant church – an ongoing collective community of God's people –

he then speaks of the "Keys of the kingdom of heaven." He insists that what is 'bound' on earth will be 'bound' in heaven, and what is 'loosed' on earth will be 'loosed' in heaven (Matt. 18: 19; cf. 18: 15-17). During the days between resurrection Sunday and Pentecost, Jesus re-taught the disciples about the kingdom of God for 40 days, with 10 days left to the 120 to seek the Lord for the coming of the Spirit (Acts 1: 14). They were 'all together in one place' (Acts 2: 1) and remained so after the Spirit descended and they were 'all filled with the Spirit and they spoke in tongues' (Acts 2: 4; 44, 46). This togetherness is more than being physically present with each other, it also means they were of one mind, one in the Spirit, for they were united in Christ. God's church was alive and would continue to expand exponentially across the Roman Empire and beyond from generation to generation. This view may not be given the acceptance it deserves, but it does seem more credible than some of the views that have been voiced. The Gospel accounts are the settings into which the Acts of the Apostles fits for they provide a background, in preparation for the arrival of the New Age of the Spirit.

If it is none of these, then we have to admit that we just do not know what 'receiving the Spirit' meant in the Upper Room. It is worth noting that Jesus did not baptise the 120 until he had been exalted to the right hand of the Father after the Ascension (Acts 1: 33) – it was only then that he sent the Spirit on the Feast of Pentecost. At the same time the Holy Spirit makes the resurrected Christ real, for throughout his ministry on earth, he was the Spirit anointed man, and now they see him as the Holy One – the great 'I AM' – who as man returns to his Father at the Ascension. He will be leaving behind a motley crew who Jesus believed in, and would in one day, fifty days later, drench or baptise them in the Spirit as the Risen and Exalted Christ.

Reflection

It is Saturday in a town in Malaysia and a local gospel church hit the streets to share the good news of salvation. They visit the places they knew – the drug dens, the drinking houses, the private clubs (brothels), the 'poverty' hovels simply to offer hope to 'captive' people. There were over one hundred and fifty people, broken down into teams, who roam the areas as they meet, pray and offer another way of life. This large community church has been doing this for years, and will continue with this weekly ministry into the distant future. Why, well many of the people in the church had come from the same background – they knew and understood what they faced. As they worked through these difficult areas – some controlled by outside forces – and many subject to demon possession. Yet, time and again, this Community Church, in dependence on the Spirit of God, ventured into hostile territory to bring peace and offer life change through prayer, the laying on of hands, and casting our evil spirits – to the glory of God. This brief analysis was given to me by the Pastoral Leader of the church I met at a Conference. This story in the Far East is not a one-off, but common practice among churches from all networks. What is true in South Asia is also true in Argentina, Brazil and in many other South American nations. Equally, the same kind of gospel work is to be found in South Africa – where we have relatives – in the townships, and is also true of Nigeria, and other parts of Africa. Churches in parts of Europe, including the UK, are also engaging in contact evangelism among groups who are the 'forgotten people'. 'is now more common for church groups to go in faith, into enemy territory and proclaim Christ in the power of the Spirit, releasing people from sickness, the occult, demon possession and other forms of spiritual captivity. Yet, glaringly still, many evangelical churches which ticks the box of spiritual mainstream ministry seem, on the face of it, to be powerless so often to break down the barriers of indifference, lack of faith and the ponderous way church is done week after week. Now, before I get my knuckles rapped, or emails hitting my in-box, or other digital approaches I am fully aware of churches in western areas where such ministries do occur – and I praise God for that.

There does need to be much more of this for UK churches – for far too long – 'charismatic churches' have been enjoying a continued love-in for themselves, instead of grasping the opportunities that are still available today. I say this in the light of a move to cancel 'conversion therapy' in the UK through legislation being considered by parliamentarians which could, if certain anti-Christian activists persist, cancel prayer, preaching, talking openly about faith and stopping literature being published (see the Christian Institute site). Hopefully, it won't happen, but MP's are not known for their spiritual erudition. Time stands still for no-one – and certainly not for the Church of God – so opportunity is the key – use it or lose it!

Spiritual Authority

The Four Gospels are the good news of the kingdom of God for they embody the truths that carry the message to the hearts, minds and wills of the people – both in the kingdom and those yet to enter God's rule and reign. The dynamic behind teaching the Word and the practical demonstration of that Word, is due to the ministry of the Holy Spirit. In our survey of the work of the Spirit in the Gospels his activity is profound. Fundamentally, the Holy Spirit is committed to the development of the proclamation of the good news and to building the life of believers. He is the person who works across the spectrum of God's new people, and makes the truths come alive in such a way that people's lives are changed and transformed. The Holy Spirit was a people-changer in the days of the first believers – and he is a still a people-changer in today's modern cultures. Re-birth, as defined in John chapter three, points to the variableness of the way the Holy Spirit operates, for he is as free as the wind – the Ruach of God. That freedom operates in partnership with the other members of the Godhood – the Father and the Son. Given that, it is surely appropriate to ask to what extent believers enjoy and trust the movement of the Spirit in their lives and churches? I say that in light of the challenges individual Christians and the corporate church face in our contemporary global society. The challenges today are much more aggressive than they have been for some time, despite the fact that God's church continues to grow at pace across the planet. Just one fact should help us to re-focus our faith and prayers across the nations, as we continue to witness aggressive hostility and physical and mental torture of believers exponentially. It has been estimated that something over 1 million believers have been martyred during the last 10 years. If that is true, and we believe that number is not fully accurate, we need to be alive to what is happening to God's people today. We would do well to heed the well-known words: "He (or we) who has an ear to hear, let him (us) hear what the Spirit says to the churches' (Rev. 3: 22).

PART 3
Water and Spirit – a Glorious Event

We recall Jesus opens with a stark declaration: "The time has come,' he said, 'the kingdom of God is near, repent and believe the gospel" (Mark 1: 15). The coming of the kingdom in Jesus was the setting in which to counter and defeat the forces of darkness and evil. One of the apostles prophetically realised the purposes of Christ's ministry: "The reason the Son of God appeared was to destroy the works of the devil" (1 John 3: 8 ESV). John the Baptist and Jesus preached about the 'reign of God' through repentance and baptism resulting in salvation (Luke 1: 69). The good news is much more than coming under God's judgement, it is about mercy, which in turn leads to being rescued and set free to enjoy God's kingly rule. The proclamation of the good news of the kingdom is an act of God. Both Jesus and the disciples had the authority to proclaim the gospel of God for the kingdom is near (Matt. 10: 7; Luke 10: 9). In fact, Jesus prophesied that:

> "this good news of the kingdom will be preached through all the world for a witness to everyone, then the end will come" (Matt. 24: 14).

In making the gospel known, Jesus encouraged his disciples to expect a response from the people who were listening to the message. For those who repented and 'received him (Jesus),'to those who believed in his name, he gave the right to become the children of God …' (John 1: 12). To be a 'child of God' is to be a 'child of the kingdom' so anyone who believed in Jesus immediately acknowledged the reign of God over their lives. The entry point into the kingdom centres on a miracle – the miracle of new life (John 10: 10) – which was confessed by believers when baptised in water.   Jesus himself underwent a miraculous baptism at the hands of his cousin, John the baptiser. The distance between the two is sharply evident, 'I Baptise with water, but he (Jesus) will baptise you with the Holy Spirit' (Mark 1: 8).   Nevertheless, Jesus entered the water, representing human sinfulness and was baptised, but in coming out of the water, the heavens opened, the

Spirit descended on him like a dove and the voice of his Father said, "You are my beloved Son; in you I take great delight" (Mark 1: 9-11). Jesus, now anointed by the Spirit, immediately began his public ministry. From then on baptism by immersion in water, after repentance, was part of the gospel message of Christ and the apostolic band. Prior to his Ascension to his Father Jesus commissioned his disciples:

> "Full authority in heaven and on earth has been given to me. Go therefore to all nations and make them my disciples; baptise them in the name of the Father, and the Son and the Holy Spirit, and teach them to observe all that I have commanded you. I will be with you always, to the end of time" (Matt. 28: 18-20).

Although water is never mentioned in the commission, it is implied for Jesus offered himself as a model to follow by believers, when they placed their faith in him for Salvation. The baptism of believers by immersion in water is practised by many different church networks across the world. I have been party to believers' baptism in the UK, USA, Israel and the Middle East, and most have been an enriching experience for those baptised and for the watching witnesses. The impact on the person baptised, on family, friends and visitors leave lasting impressions - impressions that often lead to further personal faith encounters. Baptism in water can take place in a baptismal pool in a church, a river, the sea or a swimming pool. Baptisms are usually in the setting of worship, so a sense of the presence of the Spirit pervades the atmosphere of the celebration taking place. Joy and thanksgiving are prominent, as are testimonies by the people being baptised, and normally a message of salvation precedes the baptisms – it is an occasion not to be missed.

Two Baptisms in different Nations

A Baptism for Iranians (Persia)

Christians in the West often take their 'freedoms' for granted, but for some Christians those freedoms are limited. This is certainly true for

Christians in the Middle East and North Africa where there are many restrictions. Those restrictions may apply to many areas, including, job opportunities, limited university placements, registering of churches and sudden police raids. One nation where the restrictions are severe is in the nation of Iran, the largest Eurasian population in the Middle East. Despite the restrictions, the Iranian house church movement has been growing exponentially over the last thirty years. It is estimated that there are over 100,000 Farsi house churches in the nation. In 2009, the Iranian house churches wanted to have a baptismal service for people who had come to faith in Christ. Had they tried to hold such a service in Iran they would have been arrested and imprisoned. Eventually, after much prayer and leading by the Spirit, they arranged to travel to another nation bordering Iran, to hold a baptismal service. They hired a swimming pool for the baptisms, and alongside those being baptised took friends and family. Some 246 believers (both women and men) were baptised by immersion in the pool – it was a glorious day full of praise and thanksgiving. The dress code for the baptismal was white garments. This linked the Iranian believers to the way baptisms were performed in the early centuries of the eastern Christian Church. The baptismal service was sponsored by Elam Ministries who estimated that it was probably the largest baptismal service in the Iranian churches for centuries. Iran is a Muslim nation, and people can pay a heavy price for rejecting Islam to follow Christ – sometimes with their life – whether in Iran or in some other Muslim nation. Such an event, as this was, whenever and wherever held, be it in a church, a river, a sea or a swimming pool, is always an amazing gospel opportunity. (Iran 30, Elam Ministries).

A Baptism in Israel

While on an educational visit to Israel in the 1990's I happened to be part of a group of secondary school teachers – mostly Heads of Religious Educational Departments – who spent ten days in Israel. We were touring various areas and had reached the part of the river Jordan, reputed to be the place where Jesus had been baptised by John the Baptist. Most of my colleagues had decided, it being very hot and we had travelled across Israel for some hours, to relax in a cafe. I took the opportunity to walk to the river and to the supposed site of Jesus' baptism. As I neared the river, I could hear singing and laughter, and realised there was a baptismal service taking place. The people were praising God in another language – Portuguese. Though familiar with some of the language, having been to Brazil, I found myself talking to one of the leaders – in English, thankfully. The group were from a Pentecostal Church, which had suggested the possibility of having the baptisms in Israel. The people responded in large numbers and that day some 200 hundred people – plus family and friends – were present for a life-affirming believers' water baptism in the river Jordan. It was a truly inspiring occasion with purposeful worship, the gospel proclaimed, singing in the Spirit, prophetic words and some, having been anointed in the Spirit, spoke in tongues. It was a privilege to be present on such an occasion and to join in the praise and worship. What a memorable day!

Two memorable believer's baptisms in two different nations, highlighting the way the gospel of the cross and resurrection had impacted the lives of many people. Both were glorious events, for those being baptised and for the witnesses - usually families and friends. It's always an amazing spectacle.

Believer's Baptism by Water

Baptism by water is regarded by some biblical scholars as a sacrament, while others speak of it as an ordinance, by which personal faith in Jesus is sealed by water. Whatever the view, and there are those who refer to baptism in water by immersion as both a sacrament and an ordinance. You can take your pick, either way it is a core belief and is a vital sign of new found faith in Christ. Throughout the New Testament, the mode is always by immersion in water. The Greek word 'baptizo' (used 80 times) means 'to plunge, to dip, to immerse,' and pictures someone who is a believer being plunged into the water as an act of faith. Two immediate examples are found in the Synoptic Gospels. According to Mark people were baptised by John the Baptist 'in' (Gk: en) the river Jordan (1: 5). And when Jesus was baptised he 'came up out of' (Gk: ek) the river Jordan (1: 10). In the Gospel of John we are informed that the Baptist baptised near 'Aenon because there was much water there' (3: 23). Some churches have another form of baptism for infants, where spink-ling is used with water with the sign of the cross, but there is no New Testament textual evidence for this kind of baptism. Rumours of infant baptism are no earlier than the 2nd century AD by Tertullian (c. 200), and he was against it! The argument for infant baptism is fraught with inconsistencies when trying to justify the baptism of infants. I respect the churches who favour this form of baptism, but regard it as an imported church act outside the boundaries of the teaching of the Scriptures.

> Over thirty passages in the New Testament are about believer's baptism in water by immersion, which was regarded as an essential part in gospel proclamation by the early church. We will, in the course of our study, examine what water baptism means for the people of God. In the meantime, just to give some flavour of the importance of believer's baptism using the 'it' pronoun as means of focus:

> It is about the Lordship of Christ. It is a call to follow Jesus and obey his demands. It is a gospel command and is part of the good news. It is about the kingdom of God. It is a response to the gospel through an act of faith. It is a symbol pointing to a transformed life. It is about washing and being clean. It is about death and resurrection. It is an act of repentance, preceded by confession, leading to forgiveness. It is a sign that the baptised have fallen in love with Jesus. It is a relationship with the Saviour. It is proof that a person has transferred from the kingdom of darkness into the kingdom of God. It is covenantal in its effect on believers. It is a core belief. It is always linked to the work of the Holy Spirit.

Every baptism in the book of Acts took place after the gospel message was believed. This was the standard, for there were no un-baptised Christians in the Early Church. Baptism was never an optional extra – to pick or to leave! Believer's baptism by immersion in water is a command to follow, confirming that believers are willing to be disciples' of Christ. Above all, believer's baptism is a baptism into Christ (Gk: en

Christos). Baptism is not the end of the road; it is the beginning of the end; it is the start of a new kingdom lifestyle that continues through time into eternity.

In order to have some clarity on the significance of believer's baptism in the New Testament, I have listed the textual passages referring to baptism in the Gospels, Acts and the Letters. There will then be a deeper background story behind the many different baptisms in the New Testament books. It is worth stating, to avoid confusion, when it comes to the Spirit that the Gospel is about something that will happen, Acts is about something that is happening and the Letters is about something that has happened (D. Pawson, Sovereign World, 1992, 39). For ease of understanding the baptismal texts are listed from the different books in the New Testament:

The Gospels

John said, I baptise with water, but he will baptise you with the Holy Spirit. At that time Jesus came from Nazareth in Galilee and was baptised by John in the river Jordan. As Jesus was coming out of the water, he saw the heaven being torn open and the Spirit descending on him like a dove. And a voice came from heaven: "You are my Son, whom I love; with you I am well pleased" (Mark 1: 9).

> 'I baptise you with water for repentance. But after me will come one who is more powerful than I ... He will baptise with the Hoy Spirit and with fire Then Jesus came from Galilee to the Jordan to be baptised by John. But John deterred him, saying I need to be baptised by you, ... then John consented. As soon as Jesus was baptised he went up out of the water. At that moment heaven was opened, and he saw the Spirit descending like a dove and lighting on him. And a voice came from heaven said, "This is my Son, whom I love; with him I am well pleased' (Matt. 3: 11-16).

> 'When all the people were baptized, Jesus was baptised too. And as he was praying, heaven was opened and the Holy Spirit descended on him in bodily form like a dove. And a

voice came from heaven: "You are my Son, whom I love; with whom I am well pleased" (Luke 3: 1).

"I baptise with water," John replied, "but among you stands one who you do not know. He is the one who comes after me ... Look, the Lamb of God, who takes away the sin of the world! ... The man whom you see the Spirit come down and remain is he who will baptise with the Holy Spirit" (John 1: 16, 29, 33).

Jesus said, 'I tell you the truth, no one can see the kingdom of God unless he is born of water and the Spirit. Flesh gives birth to flesh, but the Spirit gives birth to Spirit' (John 3: 5)

The Acts

"Repent and be baptised every one of you in the name of Jesus Christ for the forgiveness of your sins, and you will receive the gift of the Holy Spirit. For the promise is for you and for your children and for all who are afar off, everyone whom the Lord our God calls to himself"(Acts 2: 38-39). "Those who accepted the message were baptised, about three thousand were added to their number that day" (Acts 2: 41).

"... they believed Philip as he preached the good news of the kingdom of God and the name Jesus Christ, they were baptised, both men and women" (Acts 8: 12). "When the apostles ... arrived, they prayed for them that they might receive the Holy Spirit, because the Holy Spirit had not yet come upon any of them; they had simply been baptised into the name of the Lord Jesus" (Acts 8: 15-16).

Philip told the Ethiopian Chancellor 'the good news about

Jesus' and the Eunuch said, "Look, here is water why shouldn't I be baptised? Then both Philip and the Eunuch went down into the water and Philip baptized him. When they came up out of the water, the Spirit of the Lord suddenly took Philip away …"(Acts 8: 36-39).

"Brother Saul, the Lord Jesus,… has sent me (Ananias) so that you may see again and be filled with the Holy Spirit, immediately, … he could see again. He got baptised, and after taking some food, he regained his strength" (Acts 9: 17-19).

"While Peter was still speaking these words, the Holy Spirit came on all who heard the message … for they heard them speaking in tongues and praising God… So he ordered that they be baptised in the name of Jesus Christ" (Acts 10: 44, 47-48).

"One of those listening was a woman named Lydia, a dealer in purple cloth… who was a worshipper of God. The Lord opened her heart to respond to Paul's message. When she and the members her household were baptised, she invited us to her home" (Acts 16: 14-15).

Paul, responding to the Jailor's cry said, "Believe on the Lord Jesus Christ – you and your household … immediately he and all his family were baptised'" (Acts 16: 31, 33).

"Paul told the people to believe … in Jesus. On hearing this, they were baptised into the name of the Lord Jesus' When he placed his hands on them, the Holy Spirit came on them, and they spoke in tongues and prophesied" (Acts 19: 4-6).

The Apostolic Letters

"Is Christ divided? Was Paul crucified for you? Were you baptised into the name of Paul? I am thankful that I did not baptise any of you except Crispus and Gaius, so no one can say that you were baptised into my name. Yes, I also baptised the household of Stephanos; beyond that, I don't remember if I baptised anyone else" (1 Cor. 1: 15-16).

"For we were all baptised by one Spirit into the body of Christ – whether Jews or Greeks, slave or free – and were all given the one Spirit to drink" (1 Cor. 12: 13).

'Now if there is no resurrection, what will those do who are baptised for the dead? If the dead are not raised at all, why are people baptised for them' (Acts 15: 29).

"You are all sons of God through faith in Christ Jesus, for all of you who were baptised into Christ have clothed yourselves with Christ. There is neither Jew nor Greek, slave nor free, male nor female, for you are all one in Christ Jesus" (Gal. 3: 26-27).

"There is one body and one Spirit – just as you were called to one hope when you were called – one Lord, one faith, one baptism; one God and Father of us all, ... " (Eph. 4: 4-5). "Husbands love you wives, just as Christ loved the church and gave himself up for her to make her holy, cleansing her by the washing with water through the word ..." (Eph. 5: 25-26).

"In him you were also circumcised, in the putting off of the sinful nature, not with circumcision done by the hands of men but with the circumcision done by Christ, having been buried with him in baptism and raised with him through your faith in the power of God, who raised him from the dead" (Col. 2: 11-12).

"Therefore let us leave the elementary teachings about Christ and go on to maturity, not laying again the foundation of repentance ... instruction about baptisms ..." (Heb. 6: 1-2).

"In the days of Noah, 'only a few people, eight in all, were saved through water, and this water symbolises baptism that now saves you – not the removal of dirt from the body but the pledge of a good conscience toward God. It saves you by the resurrection of Jesus Christ, ... " (1 Peter 3: 20-21).

"This is the one who came by water and blood – Jesus Christ. He did not come by water only, but by water and blood. And in the Spirit who testifies, because the Spirit is the truth. For there are three that testify: the Spirit, the water and the blood; and the three are in agreement" (1 John 5: 6-8).

"What shall we say, then? Shall we go on sinning so that grace may increase? By no means! We died to sin; how can we live in it any longer? Or don't you know that all of us who were baptised into Christ Jesus were baptised into his death. We were therefore buried with him through baptism into death in order that just as Christ was raised from the dead through the glory of the Father, we too may live a new life" (Rom 6: 1-4).

The Core Elements of Believers Baptism

The Pentecost Baptism

On the Feast of Pentecost, in the city of Jerusalem in AD 29, the Holy Spirit fell upon the 120 disciples in the Upper Room. As believers, they had prayed 24/7 for the promise of the Father to come upon them and, on the very Day of the Feast they were baptized in the Spirit – filled to overflowing (Acts 2: 4). Such was the commotion with the sound of the wind of God – the Ruach – blowing over them, the fire of the Spirit resting upon them, that they praised him in tongues (Acts 2: 1-4). At some point they staggered into the streets full of the Spirit, declaring 'the wonders of God' in many languages. The crowds were amazed at what they saw and heard and regarded the disciples as being like drunk men and women, wondering what 'this meant' (Acts 2: 5-13). It is very likely that the disciples, moved into the Temple area to accommodate the large crowds, in all probably, Solomon's Porch (now the Al Aqsa Mosque)

The apostle Peter preached to the Diaspora Jews and the local communities, explaining that the Last Days had arrived, as predicted in the Old Testament Scriptures (Joel 2: 28-32; Psalm 16: 8-11; 110: 1). He then proclaimed the gospel of the kingdom of God to the 'captured audience' and spoke of the cross of Jesus, the gift of the Spirit and the Resurrection of Christ (Acts 2: 17-36). The response of the crowd was to cry out for help. Peter then challenged them to "save yourselves from this corrupt generation" (Acts 2: 40) and respond to the message:

> "Repent and be baptised every one of you in the name of Jesus Christ for the forgiveness of your sins, and you will receive the gift of the Holy Spirit. For the promise is for you and for your children and for all who are afar off – for everyone whom the Lord our God calls to himself" (Acts 2: 38-39 ESV).

The outcome of Peter's appeal led 3000 men to repent, believe, receive forgiveness of their sins, and experience the gift of the Spirit. According to Luke they were baptised by immersion in water (Acts 2: 41), in all probability in the mikveh pools adjacent to the Temple. Some days or weeks later, as Peter and John went to pray in the Temple, a physically impaired beggar pleaded for help. He was healed through the action of the apostles, as they shouted "In the name of Jesus of Nazareth, walk" (Acts 3: 6). The man then proceeded to run through the Temple courts, "walking and leaping and praising God" (Acts 3: 3-11). Confounded by this strange sight, by a man many of them knew as a beggar, people gathered in Solomon's Colonnade in the Temple grounds and Peter, seeing an opportunity, preached to the crowds about Jesus as the Christ, crucified and risen, but present by his Spirit, based on prophecy from the Old Testament. Even though the authorities intervened, some 5,000 men, "heard their message, believed" (Acts 3: 1-4: 5). The author of Acts does not record the baptisms of the 5,000, but it would be unthinkable not to baptise them, for that was the means whereby people entered into the community of God's kingdom people in Jerusalem – the church. One added feature of the 'new' community was that they appear to have taken over Solomon's Colonnade as their regular meeting place, constantly attracting people from beyond Jerusalem due to their lifestyle, ministry, healing and charismatic worship (Acts 5: 12-16).

Doctor Luke then provides us with a bird's eye view of the way the message of the good news of the kingdom of God was proclaimed across the Roman Empire. The gospel was preached to people individually and to crowds. This was done by the apostolic band and by other disciples as they travelled between towns and cities. Time and again we are shown the nature of the proclamation and the demonstration of the good news. The pattern they used was similar to the time they had with Jesus prior to his death and resurrection. They followed Jesus' instructions to the letter due to the authority he imparted to them:

> "When Jesus had called the twelve together, he gave them power and authority to drive out all demons and to cure diseases, and he sent them out to proclaim the kingdom of God and to heal the sick" (Luke 9: 1-2).

Their ability and authority was obviously quickened post-Pentecost because of their empowerment by the HolySpirit, for there was now no limit to where they went. True, the sudden rise of persecution did mean that the church in Jerusalem was facing considerable challenges, but the apostles and disciples carried through their mandate (Acts 4:-5: 21; 5: 17-40; 6: 8-8: 3; Matt. 28: 19-20). Notably, in the middle of the constant interference of the Jewish authorities, the apostles and disciples for they "cannot help speaking about what they have seen and heard" (Acts 4: 20). They rejoiced that they had been counted worthy to suffer 'in disgrace for the Name,' day after day, in the Temple courts and from house to house, they never stopped teaching and proclaiming the good news that Jesus is the Messiah (Acts 5: 41-42). One other tangible element as part of their given 'resources' was prayer, for their ministry was born in prayer, mirrored by Jesus himself, and was a constant means of support as they pursued their calling (Acts 1: 14; 24; 2: 42; 4: 24; 31; 6: 6; et al).

Reflection

Any reading of the Gospel and Acts points to a God who is both immanent and transcendent, for he is both with us and beyond us. To introduce God to year 7 pupils in the Secondary School, most of whom were un-churched, I decided with my RE staff to use C.S. Lewis's story of the Lion, the Witch and the Wardrobe. One particular part of the story was the discussion between Lucy and Susan, who were trying to understand what Aslan was like. Aslan, symbolises the Son of God, so when Lucy asked, 'Is – he a man?' 'Aslan a man!' said Mr Beaver sternly. 'Certainly not. I tell you he is the King ... and the son of the Emperor-Beyond-the-Sea ...Aslan is a lion – the lion, the great Lion.' 'Ooh!' said Susan, 'I'd thought he was a man. Is he – quite safe? 'Safe?' said Mr Beaver. 'Who said anything about safe? Course he isn't safe. But he's good. He's the King, I tell you.' (Collins, 1981, 77). They understood the symbolism and began to see that God is good, but also that he isn't safe – he is different, he is Lord and greater than human beings. The classes had, with some guidance, to write up a tabloid about what they thought God was like – they had to imagine that God existed. It was not just a fun time, but through the learning they did some group graphics and drawings, without being told, of the attributes of God. At the next lesson we had open debates on the existence of God, and if he/she did exist, what was she/he like? The final outcome was to look at the Bible and do some research about God. For modern believers, there are times when God is far too immanent – almost matey – or too severe – too distant. Thankfully, in the Gospels and Acts we see both sides of the character of God – immanent and transcendent, but most of all personal. The children enjoyed the adventure! What an amazing God we have.

Snapshots – Other Water Baptisms in Acts

Acts, as a record of God's first churches in the Middle East and Europe, covered a period of some thirty years, from AD 29-AD 60. Luke, who must have kept his reed-pen ready for any eventualities, put on record what he saw and witnessed. Initially, he kept a 'diary' of Peter's apostolic ministry and some events surrounding other members of his team. When Paul, with Barnabas, began to form another apostolic team, he changed tack and followed the expanding ministry of the apostle Paul. The 'silence' about what was happening with other apostolic teams is one of the mysteries of the book of Acts. We know that Luke covered both apostles, for the 'we' passages have identified Luke as one of the travelling companions of both men. It is now appropriate to view the other accounts when water baptism was part of a Gospel event. We will briefly cover seven of the stories recorded by the author, when people and communities, faced with the gospel of the kingdom, responded in faith to become followers of Christ. The records of Luke, over three decades covers the areas of Jerusalem, Judea, Samaria and parts of the European mainland (Acts 1-8). Alongside the proclamation of the kingdom message, were fierce persecution, riots, imprisonment, beatings and hostility by Jewish leaders, town councils, and local business leaders against Christians and churches. Yet, by the 4th century AD, Christianity had become the religion of the Roman Empire!

Philip in Samaria and Gaza (Acts 8: 1-39)

Philip, having emerged from 'the great persecution' in Jerusalem, was one of those who 'scattered' to other areas under the direction of the Holy Spirit. A man, full of the Spirit and wisdom, a servant (Gk: diaconia) – who ministered to Hebrew women, but was also an evangelist (Acts 6: 1-7). He fervently preached the 'word of the gospel,' proclaimed the Messiah, drew crowds, and became involved in signs and wonders. He saw many captive people set free from evil spirits, for the paralysed and the lame were healed and there was great joy in the Samaria (8: 1-8). Among those who believed was Simon, known as a sorcerer, but seeing Philip's power from above, he realise he could not compete. He was then baptised, but was so taken up with Philip that he followed him "everywhere astonished by the great signs and miracles" (8: 13). The Jerusalem team of Peter and John arrived in the city, having heard the good news about Philip's ministry, but noticed they had not yet received the Spirit. Immediately they acted, laid hands on them, and they were all filled with the Spirit. Simon, seeing this, wanted the same, only to be rebuked by Peter who warned him about his deceitful and wicked heart. At which point Simon pleaded for 'grace' and though nothing else is said by Luke there is every possibility that Simon was given a reprieve after repentance (8: 24). The baptism did take place in water by immersion not just for Simon but for others who professed to believe in Jesus as Messiah.

The Ethiopian Chancellor (8: 26-39)

An angel now directs Philip and moves him towards Gaza, in the south of Israel. On the way he bumps into an Ethiopian Eunuch, the Chancellor of the Queen of the Ethiopians, who was returning from Jerusalem after worshipping in the Temple in the city. Had he been present on the Day of Pentecost, or heard about this new 'religion' and strange stories of people being healed? We have no idea, but this was a divine moment, for Philip was directed by the Spirit to speak boldly to this distinguished traveller. The Ethiopian was reading some scrolls of the Old Testament. Philip may well have had a double take, because here was a man on the way back to his country, reading a Messianic passage from the book of the prophet Isaiah. Confused by the reading he allowed Philip to explain the meaning of "He was led like a sheep to the slaughter, and as a Lamb before its shearer is silent, so he did not open his mouth ..." (Isa. 53: 7-8; 8: 26-33). The Eunuch, full of questions, listened to Philip as he explained the meaning, pointed him to the Messiah-Christ and explained the Gospel of the kingdom and the need for belief and baptism. As they continued to travel, the Eunuch spots some water and asks to be baptised, which Philip does. No sooner is he baptised by immersion and coming up out of the water, than the evangelist is taken away by the Spirit, allowing the chancellor to go on his way rejoicing' (8: 30-39).

Damascus and Saul (Acts 9: 1-19)

The Damascus Road incident, when Saul met Jesus face to face, is one of the great stories of personal confrontation that leads eventually to transformation. The details of the event have been shared by Saul to Luke who, describes as best he can, the revelation he received. Saul, headstrong as ever is searching for the Lord's disciples, as he 'breathes out threats' to the followers of the Nazarene. A light from heaven stops him in his tracts, blinds him and, falling to the ground off his horse, he hears a voice: "Saul, Saul, why do you persecute me?" (9: 4). To persecute Christians is to persecute the Lord of Glory. Saul responds, 'Who are you, Lord?' brings an immediate reply: 'I am Jesus whom you are persecuting' go into Damascus and you will be guided as you enter the city. It is noticeable that Saul does not react to this sudden and dramatic change in his journey – he knows who Jesus is – the crucified, risen and ascended Messiah-Christ. The shock must have been all consuming as he lay on the ground trying to figure out what had happened to him. Meanwhile, a disciple of Christ called Ananias had a vision of Jesus, who instructs him to go to a house in 'Straight Street' in the city where he will find Saul, praying. Somewhat taken aback, he protests, but given assurances that Saul is a 'chosen instrument' for both Gentiles and Jews, the disciple makes his way to the house where the persecutor is staying. Ananias 'lays hands on Saul,' heals his eyes and anoints him with the Holy Spirit. This Pentecostal baptism seems to energise Saul, and he is taken to some water (implied) and is baptised by immersion, confirming he has transferred from the kingdom of darkness and the power of Satan, into the family of God (26: 18). Saul, who became known as Paul (Greek name), never got over what happened to him on the way to Damascus and later wrote about it in a letter to churches in Galatia: 'I have been crucified by Christ and I no longer live, but Christ lives in me. The life I live in the body, I live by faith in the Son of God, who loved me and gave himself for me' (Gal. 2: 20).

The Centurion, Cornelius in Caesarea (Acts 10: 23-48)

Cornelius, a Roman centurion based in Caesarea, a 'God-fearing man' known for his charitable work among the poor of the population. Within his home, he is faced with an angel visitor who informs him that his prayers have been answered. He is instructed to send for a man, Simon Peter by name, who is staying in Joppa. Servants are despatched to find him as Cornelius awaits the outcome of a meeting that will transform the community. Prior to the arrival of the delegation from Caesarea, Peter is praying on the roof of the house where he is staying and receives a revelation from God. The unusual 'dream' is strange as it includes a huge sheet being let down from heaven to earth, containing kosher and non-kosher animals and Peter is commanded to eat them. He protests that he has not eaten anything impure or unclean (non-kosher food), but the Lord makes it clear that he is "not to call anything impure that God has made clean" (10-1-15). The vision is repeated three times as the apostle ponders the meaning of the revelation he has received. His reverie is interrupted by his host who informs him that three men have come to speak with him from the home of Cornelius, a Centurion. The Spirit confirms to Peter that this is a 'God moment' and he engages with the men, has them hosted as guests, and travels with the men the next day to Caesarea (10: 16-22). At the Gentile Centurion's home, Peter acknowledges that it was not proper for a Jew to visit a non-Jew (Heb. Goyem, Gentile) in their home, because it went against Jewish tradition. Yet, due to a vision from God, the apostle understood that such a tradition no longer applied. He was free to be entertained in the house of Cornelius. The Centurion explained to the apostle that he only sent for him, because 'a man in shining clothes' appeared to him in a dream and asked him to make contact with him in Joppa. Peter apologises for his original truculence, and immediately seizes the opportunity to explain the Gospel to the Centurion (10: 23-35). The evangelist reminds his audience that God's message is 'good news of peace through Jesus Christ, who is Lord of all' (10: 36). Peter offers a summary of the good news: "God anointed Jesus of Nazareth with the Holy Spirit and power, and how he went about doing good and healing all who were under the power of the devil, because God was with him" (10: 38). The testimony of the team, as witnesses of those events, is that this same Jesus was crucified, but "God raised him from the dead on the third day and was seen by many people after his resurrection" (10: 40). As Peter was speaking, 'the Holy Spirit came on all who heard the message' which surprised the Jewish people present because the Spirit was poured out on the Gentiles, who spoke in tongues and praised God. It was only after this that they "were baptised in the name of Jesus Christ" (10: 44-48). Again, this is a reminder that both the coming of the Spirit and believer's baptism in water by immersion was part of the package. To all intents and purposes, the church in the Centurion's house was the first Gentile church.

Philippi –the First European Church (Acts 16: 11-34)

Paul and his team were determined to go to the provinces of Phrygia, Galatia and Bithynia, but each time they were thwarted from going to those areas by the Holy Spirit. As they waited on the Lord in Troas, Paul was given a vision of a man from Macedonia begging for help, so it was to Europe that Paul and his missionary team travelled (16: 6-10).

Lydia and the Jailor (16: 11-34)

On reaching the Roman city of Philippi, Paul and Silas went to the city gate by the river and, while there, met with some 'praying' women. One of the women was a business person named Lydia, who dealt in purple cloth from Thyatira. She was a worshipper of God. The Gospel of the kingdom opened her heart and "she and members of her household were baptised,'" probably in the nearby river. The team,who were invited into her home, which may have become a base for the 'church in her house.' Paul and Silas used the river meeting place for prayer as a focus for contacting people from the township. It was while they were using the site, that they were accosted by a slave girl who kept following the team. She seemed to be a fortune-teller, predicting people's futures events in their lives, but for some unknown reason kept following the missionaries. As she did, she shouted constantly, 'these men are the servants of the Most High God, telling you the way of salvation (16: 17). True to fact, she was in league with some business men who grew rich on her occult skills. For the most part she was ignored by the missionary team, but eventually Paul had had enough; spoke to the spirit driving the girl, "In the name of Jesus Christ I command you to come out of her" (16: 18). Once the girl was freed from the spirit that possessed her, the owners discovered their finances were no longer what they were! In their fury they dragged Paul and Silas before local magistrates who had them stripped, beaten and thrown into Prison. The Jailer, under direction, placed them in a cell with their feet in the stocks (16: 19-24).Paul and Silas, unfazed by what had happened, started a praise meeting at midnight, by singing songs and praying. In the midst of the praise time, there was an earthquake, which caused the prison doors to fly open and the chains holding the prisoners became loose. When the jailor realised all the prison doors were open, he grabbed a sword to commit suicide, but was stopped by Paul and Silas. The prisoners were still in their cells, and the confused jailor, responsible for the prisoners, fell trembling before Paul. He shouted: 'Sirs, what must I do to be saved?' (16: 25-30). The reply was blunt: "Believe on the Lord Jesus Christ, and you will be saved – you and your household" (16: 31). Paul and Silas continued to preach the 'word of the Lord' to the jailors family and the men in the cells. With the wounds washed by the jailor who, with his family believed, and were then baptised into Christ. Inevitably, Paul with Silas, probably kept to the same mantra as the other apostles (Acts 2: 38). The two men were fed by the man, who demanded that the magistrates come personally to release them from prison because they were Roman citizens. They made their way to Lydia's home where they encouraged the believers (16: 31-30). Some bible teachers view the 'household baptisms' as justification for young children being baptised as infants. Even if that were so, they would have to believe before their baptism.

To argue for Infant Baptism here, is an argument from silence, which is weak and without justification.

Ephesus (Acts 19: 1-7)

On arriving in Ephesus, Paul met some men who claimed to be disciples, to whom the apostle asked a question: 'Did you receive the Holy Spirit when or after you believed? (19: 2). The word 'disciple' is generally only used of followers of Jesus in Acts, though some teachers argue that it could easily refer to followers of John the Baptist. It is important to bear in mind that this is probably some twenty years after the death of John the Baptist, and to find a group of his followers so far from Judea seems unlikely. Nevertheless, it does appear that what the apostle asked was to dig out where the men stood in regard to their personal faith. Yes, their initial baptism was John's but then that could also be applied to some of the first followers of Jesus, who were baptised by John. The baptism of John was a baptism of repentance and was far from adequate, for he even pointed away from himself to 'the one coming after him, that is, Jesus' (19: 4). When Paul realised they lacked any knowledge about the Spirit, and that their baptism was faulty, "they were baptised into the name of the Lord Jesus"(19: 5). Again, as before, this would be as believers and by immersion somewhere in a nearby pool or river. Whatever we may think of this baptism into Christ, this was a second baptism for these twelve men, superior in kind to the baptism of John. For Paul to pursue the 're-baptism' of these men goes against the grain of most modern biblical scholars today, but then the apostle was not subject to modern 'political' niceties. It does raise the question as to whether those who were baptised as babies, and have come to an understanding of believer's water baptism, should be able to go through a second baptism without much rancour. This is not the place to debate the pros and cons of infant baptism and believer's water baptism. Having baptised the men, Paul placed his hands upon them and 'the Holy Spirit came upon them, and they spoke in tongues and prophesied' (19: 6). This was an outpouring from above – from Jesus who is at the right hand of the Father – which equipped them for their ministries, and was a conscious experience for the men, confirmed by 'signs following' (19:

6). This was a 'felt' visible encounter with God, for each of the men were fully aware of all that happened to each other.

Baptism in Water - A Prophetic Explanation

In one sense there is nothing very special about being baptised in water – it is simply water that comes from our reservoirs, rivers or seas. It is not designated as holy. Yet, when water is used for baptism it takes on a new meaning, for water is used for washing, cleansing, purifying and even healing. The bible has hundreds of references to water: 'there are springs of water' (Isa. 49: 10), 'running water' (Zech. 14: 8), 'living water' (John 4: 10), 'streams of water' (John 7: 38, and 'washing with water' (Eph. 5: 26), to name but a few. To the people in Jerusalem in the time of Jesus, water was plentiful around the Temple through the mikveh pools. The huge crowds on the Church's first Pentecost, must have been witnesses to an amazing spectacle when 3,000 people believed, were baptised by/with the Spirit and immersed in water, by the apostles and disciples (Acts 2: 38, 41). The baptism of John the Baptist, who washed people in the river Jordan, must have been eclipsed when the Day of the Lord was celebrated in such a visual way. So whatever might be said about water, one thing is certain, believer's baptism in water can be, and should be, a spectacle wherever held. After all, the baptiser and the baptised should be full of praise and thanksgiving as they celebrate their new life, new name and new identity, when confessing that Jesus Christ as Lord, to the glory of God the Father. Believer's baptism is a public prophetic declaration to God in heaven, and to the witnesses on earth, that God has acted in a saving way to advance his kingdom. Believer's baptism is a global phenomenon because it signifies three theological inductive truths: the water, the blood and the Spirit, which is the testimony of God, for Christ has overcome the world (1 John 5: 7-9). Likewise, through faith in King Jesus, we have triumphed in him 'for he who has the Son has life' (1 John 5: 11-12). One writer describes the act of baptism in water:

> 'Here ... something is actually done – a step is taken that can never be retracted – something has happened, something definable, with a setting in time and space, attested by witnesses. Behind that lies ... a definitive event ...'(C.H.

Dodd), in Baptism in the New Testament, G.R. Beasley-Murray, 1962 p 235).

There is also a covenantal aspect to believer's baptism by immersion in water, due to the fact that every baptised person is automatically incorporated into God's kingdom community – the Church. This means that the Christian immediately and spontaneously belongs to a local church and the universal Church of God.

Baptism in the Apostolic Letters

In general terms, faith baptism in water is when a person is immersed in the water, signifying a death and a resurrection. In many respects it is a declaration to God, and to the 'watching world,' that such a person is serious about their intention to follow Christ – come what may. The following passages are from the Letters of Paul, Peter, John and the author of Hebrews: Romans 6: 1-12; 1 Corinthians 1: 10-17; 10: 11-15; 15: 29-30; Galatians 3: 26-27; Ephesians 4: 5; 5: 25-26; Colossians 1: 13; 2: 11-15; 2 Timothy 2: 11-13; Titus 3: 5-6; Hebrews 6: 1-6; 10: 22-23; 1 Peter 3: 18-21; 1 John 5: 5-8 (with John 3: 5-7). The Roman text will be left to the last of the eighteen Scriptural texts.

1 Corinthians

Several passages in 1 Corinthians contain insights into the way believer's baptism is understood. One of the most important passages is 1 Corinthians 12: 13, "For we were all baptised by one Spirit into one body – whether Jews or Greeks, slaves or free – and we were all given one Spirit to drink." That text, however, is better suited to part two, Volume 2 and that somewhat contentious narrative will be considered then.

Divisions in the church (1 Cor. 1: 10-17)

The disunity in Corinth was a major issue, due in part, to the immaturity of the members of the community. Initially, Paul gave thanks to God for the fact that they 'have been enriched in every way' for their 'testimony' about Christ was due to the grace of God. They did not lack 'any spiritual gift' as they waited for 'the day of our Lord Jesus Christ' (1: 4-9). The apostle had received news from 'Chloe's household' that people had divided into four parties, including the 'Paul' party. Livid with this kind of behaviour, the apostle chastised them by asking if Christ was divided. Were they baptised into Paul? To counteract their attitudes, he pointed out that he had baptised Crispus, Gaius and the household of Stephanas, for he was sent not to baptise, but to preach the gospel, for that was his calling (1 Cor. 1: 1; 11-17). There is no sign that Paul is against baptism because during his ministry he, with the other apostles, would have been party to baptisms. It really does not matter who does the baptisms, so there is no need to talk about him as if he was some unique person – replacing Christ. The whole idea was preposterous. He urges them to come together as one family in Christ and to avoid partisanship. Believers baptism in and of itself is still a core element in following Jesus.

Warnings from History (1 Cor. 10: 1-5)

The key phrase is "they (all the Israelites) passed through the sea" for "they were all baptised into Moses in the cloud and in the sea" (1 Cor. 10: 2-3). Paul's use of the baptismal 'metaphor' appears to indicate that all the people were liberated from the pursuing Egyptian army. In essence they were led by Moses – who took them through the Red sea baptism, covered by the 'cloud' representing the presence of God. He does not make any direct link to believer's baptism, except to indicate that having been freed by the 'water' experience, they were under the judgement of God, despite drinking from the spiritual food and rock, for it was Christ who was with them. The lesson is that they failed to adhere to what God was saying, so Corinthian believers would do well to learn from the experience of Israel when things brought them into conflict with their Lord. It may well be that the Corinthians may have regarded Egypt as representing the evil forces of darkness, and their baptism into Moses, was their release into the kingdom of light. But this seems difficult to reconcile with the text, better still to admit that whatever Paul's intention was in using this image of baptism for the Corinthians, that they would change their ways and follow Christ (10: 8-10).

Baptism for the dead? (1 Cor.15: 29)

"Now if there is no resurrection, what will those do who are baptised for the dead? If the dead are not raised at all, why are people baptised for them" (15: 29) The setting of the passage is over questions raised about the resurrection of Christ. For example, "If there is no resurrection of the dead, then not even Christ has been raised" (15: 13). It appears that some believers, who were part of the Corinthian church, had not been baptised, so members if the church had volunteered to be substitutes for those believers who had died without baptism. This view of 'baptism for the dead' seems to be out of line with the general teaching surrounding baptism, and also cuts across the main teaching of Paul about the resurrection. True, there were questions raised about the resurrection of Christ in the church family, but it is believed that doubters about the resurrection came from outside the church. Paul squashed the doubters earlier in his teaching (15: 13-11). So having baptismal substitutes does not seem to be favoured by him – certainly if the same people do not believe in the resurrection. Some of the people may have been influenced by some of the Hellenistic religions who were active in the city. The apostle regards substitute baptisms as not in keeping with the way the baptism of believers is practised, and seems to be saying that there is no need for such action by other believers.

Children of God (Gal. 3: 26-29)

> The apostle Paul, writing to the churches in the Province of Galatia, encouraged the saints to regard themselves as members of the family of God – without restrictions:

> "You are all the sons/daughters of God through faith in Christ Jesus, for all of you were baptised into Christ and have clothed yourselves with Christ. There is neither Jew nor Greek, slave nor free, male nor female. For you are all one in Christ Jesus. If you belong to Christ, then you are Abraham's seed, and heirs according to the promise" (3: 36-39).

Jews and Gentiles, who are believers, were justified by faith (3: 24), and it is this faith that marks them out as 'sons of God' or 'children of God' making male and female believers co-workers for God. In terms of salvation and culture, there is no difference between male and female believers. Both sexes enjoy equally the blessings of salvation. For "All of you who were baptised into Christ have clothed yourselves with Christ" (3: 27). The Christian believer literally puts on a special 'dress code' that code being the person of Christ in his work and witness – that is what baptism means. The idea that baptism in water is of secondary importance, and nothing more than a rite of entry into the church, is detrimental to the way baptism was understood in the early church.

> 'Baptism was, in the early church, the initial and necessary response to faith' (Scot McNight, NVAC 1995, 198).

Baptism pictured the death and resurrection of Christ, for the person being baptised, died and rose in Christ, when immersed in water and from water. The symbol of baptism dramatised the transformation that had taken place in the life of the believer. It was a declaration – an announcement – a victory cry to God and to witnesses, that the person was a son, a daughter, a child of God (Rom. 8: 5). Furthermore, in putting on Christ as a garment, which may refer to the Roman toga or, better still, white clothing (common in some nations) depicting a change of nature through faith in Christ. Notably, the believers in Galatia were recipients of all the blessings through Christ alongside the blessings of the promises of God to Abraham (3: 29).

One Baptism and One Church (Eph. 4: 5; 5: 25-27)

In writing to the church or churches in Ephesus, Paul presents his readers with some core values, or a confessional creed or a statement of faith:

> "Make every effort to keep the unity of the Spirit through the bond of peace. There is only one body and one Spirit, just as you were called to one hope, when you were called – one Lord, one faith, one baptism, one God and Father of all, who is over all and through all and in all" (5: 3-6).

True, baptism is only mentioned once in Ephesians, whereas the word Lord is mentioned sixteen times. What is true of the early Church is that the voice of believers across the Roman Empire was the shout: 'Jesus Christ is Lord' (Rom. 10: 9-10). Yet, in some respect that would be the cry of the baptised as they rose up out of the water, to glorify God. The 'one baptism' can only be the baptism spoken of by Peter on the Day of Pentecost – the baptism of faith (Acts 2: 38). Above all, according to the apostle:

> "Christ loved the church and gave himself up for her to make her holy, cleansing her by the washing with water through the word, and to present her to himself as a radiant church, without stain or wrinkle, or any other blemish, but holy and blameless" (5: 25-27).

This is about the future glory of the church being prepared for her marriage to the Bride, who is Christ, but the phrase, 'cleansing her by washing with water through the word' is linked to baptismal teaching. Believer's baptism in water is always with reference to the redemptive death of Christ, leading to the final glory of the church – a radiant church - at the end of the Age. The church of every race, age and generation through time has been 'washed and cleansed,' in preparation for the final kingdom. This event, in time for eternity, is that the word of the Father, Son and Holy Spirit – used at baptism is confirmation of transformation through grace, by faith in the atoning work of Christ on Calvary's cross. More than baptism, it is the cross through the blood that is the place to receive cleansing, but baptism points forever to Calvary and the empty tomb. Thus believers sing:

> And can it be that I should gain an interest in the Saviour's blood? Died he for me, who caused his pain? For me, who him to death pursued? Amazing love! How can it be that Thou, my God, should die for me!
>
> John Wesley (1707-88).

Live Well – Set your Eyes on Jesus (Colossians 2: 9-15)

When the apostolic team of Paul, Silas and Timothy, pursued their calling to preach the gospel of the kingdom in Asia Minor, they constantly met opposition from Jewish zealots. It was not only that they demanded that those who were Jewish followers of Christ continue to practice circumcision, but that Gentile converts follow the same practice. For Paul this was anathema, and a denial of the gospel of grace. Having dealt with philosophy again, (2: 8) he raised the issue of circumcision.

> "In him you were also circumcised, in putting off the sinful nature, not with a circumcision done by the hands of men but with the circumcision done by Christ" (2: 11).

Jewish circumcision is a cutting away of the male foreskin, which is a physical separation. This covenantal act is no longer viable and, in any case became suspect, because many Jews were Jews in name and not in practice (Rom. 2: 28-29). What was necessary was a 'circumcision of the heart' not the body (Deut. 30: 6). In other words, they had part of the flesh cut off, but the stubbornness of the heart needed cutting out. What then does Paul mean by the 'circumcision of Christ?' (2: 11). The thrust of Paul's argument is that when Jesus died, he was cut off from his flesh – he became a dead person! "In putting off his flesh, he died to evil, he died to sin ... though he became the likeness of sinful flesh, and for sin ... he condemned sin in the flesh" (Rom. 8: 3). By dying, he was set free from the flesh, his Spirit returned to the Father, for his flesh was buried. When Christ's flesh was stripped off him on the cross, he was marked with blood. So were believers – only this time the marks in the flesh and the shedding in blood were done to Christ. When he died, we died in him. This new kind of circumcision is for both men and women who belong to Christ.

> **Reflection**
>
> The famous Chinese Christian, Watchman Nee, describes in one of his writings what happened when this truth – when Christ died I died in him – gripped his mind and heart. He leapt out of his chair in his study, ran down the stairs and

without any kind of doubt, ran into the street. With great joy he shouted to the startled crowds: 'I'm Dead!' 'I'm Dead!' The reaction was astonishment and incredulity. How can he be dead, when he is very much alive? Inevitably this kind of emotion is natural, when the reality of what God has done in Christ, takes hold of a believer. He had suddenly realised that the 'body of sin' was 'dead in Christ,' for as Christ died on the tree he took his body with him into death. What was true for Watchman Nee is equally true of all believers.

One popular teaching approach by some traditional churches is the view that baptism has replaced circumcision. The argument is based on this passage but, to be blunt, in order to make such a claim you have to enter the world of theological gymnastics. Obviously, this is the language of paedo-baptism who attempt to justify infant baptism based on this passage. The argument is tortuous and runs thus, circumcision is at eight days, so if baptism replaces circumcision, it can be used for children as for adults. Such views, to this author, are without any credence. Moving on we come to Paul's prophetic teaching about believer's water baptism:

> "Having been buried with him (Christ) in baptism, and raised with him through your faith in the power of God, who raised him from the dead" (Col. 2: 12).

This statement by the apostle Paul is one of the clearest announcements about baptism, in the New Testament. The relationship of the believer with Christ is centred on his suffering and death on Calvary's hill. As Christ died on the cross, the believer died with him in his death, for as Christ died for sin, so the believer died to the sinfulness of sin. Baptised believers relate immediately to the reconciliation Christ won for us.

> "Therefore, if anyone is in Christ, he is a new creation, the old has gone and the new has come. All this is from God who reconciled us to himself through Christ ... not counting anyone's sins against them" (2 Cor. 5: 17-19).

Dying with Christ is only one part of the picture, because as Christ rose from the dead, so baptised believers rises from death to life. Easter is not just a place in history, it is an experience – an experience rooted in the resurrection of Christ. The believer, like Christ himself, has been raised to 'newness of life' for there is always a present factor in the Easter story. This may be a past event, but it has a present reality for those baptised into Christ. Moreover, resurrection life anticipates a glorious future, "When Christ who is our life appears, then you also will appear with him in glory" (Col. 3: 4). What an amazing outcome! Notably, an 'act of faith' by the baptised believer 'in the power of God' was a seal – a seal that confirmed the veracity of the act. In other words, through faith – faith in the baptismal event in Christ – the believer is incorporated into the community of believing people – the church of God. To back up the substantial nature of the baptismal experience, the apostle Paul presented the drama of redemption by taking the readers back to Easter. He then asked the readers to visualize the crucifixion:

> You were dead in your sins because of your sinful nature
> God made you alive with Christ and forgave your sins
> The written code – the legal documents – has been cancelled
> That which was against and opposed him was taken away
> He did that by nailing it to the cross with the word 'cancelled' across it
> He disarmed the powers and authorities against him – human and satanic
> He made a public spectacle of them, triumphing over them by the cross

(Col. 2: 13-15).

Believers in Colossae, who had never seen the first Easter, were confronted with the starkness of it, but in the midst of the blackness was the light of God. For Golgotha was a triumph, and the resurrection proves that, beyond any doubt. God gave Christ a new life on Easter Day and those who are baptised in Christ have risen to a new way of living. In being 'raised with Christ' they are encouraged to 'set their hearts and minds on things above' where 'Christ is seated at the right hand of God.' Earthly things have less value than heavenly things, for they have died for 'their life is now hidden with Christ in God' (Col.3: 1-3). It is vital for believers to keep their gaze toward where Christ is seated in glory, majestic and in power, for everything that happened to Christ happened to believers.

Life that is Eternal (John 3: 1-8; 1 John 5: 5-8)

The Gospel of John and the First Letter of John are due to the quill of the apostle John, who wrote both documents. Both the Gospel and the Letter were written that the readers may know that:

> "God has given us eternal life, and this life is in his Son. He who has the Son has life; who does not have the Son of God does not have life" (cf. John 20: 21; 1 John 5: 11-12).

Eternal Life (John 3: 1-8)

The Nicodemus story gives clarity to the combination of 'water and Spirit,' in the offer of new life, for 'unless one is born of water and the Spirit,' said Jesus, 'he or she cannot enter the kingdom of God' (3: 5). There was no point in Jesus mentioning water if it did not have a connection with 'water baptism.' The theologian may well have seen John baptising people or would have heard about him, for all Judea seemed to know about his presence and practice of baptising penitents 'for the forgiveness of sin' (John 3: 3). Apart from that, as a learned scholar he would have known of the promises made of the Last Days, in which the outpoured Spirit would be prominent among the people (Ezek. 36: 36ff). The mention of water is a baptismal motif which for the priest would be necessary alongside the gift of the Spirit. Jesus plainly tells the man, that there is no entrance into the kingdom unless both are experienced. Tantalisingly, there is every possibility that Nicodemus could have been at the crucifixion of Jesus, for he was prominent at the burial of Jesus (John 19: 39). Perhaps, having seen the passion of Jesus during his last week, may have brought the

Pharisee to the point of belief, and maybe baptism six weeks later on the Day of Pentecost. Arguments from silence are not always fantasy, any more than some of the outlandish imaginative suggestions that are recorded in scholastic and theological literature, but at least there is some evidence for Nicodemus' about turn recorded in the Gospel.

The Testimony (1 John 5: 5-8)

John's testimony is about:

> "the one who came by water and the blood – Jesus Christ. He did not come by water only, but by water and blood. And it is the Spirit who testifies, because the Spirit is truth. For there are three testimonies: the Spirit, the water and the blood; these three are in agreement ... this is the testimony of God" (6-9).

The three elements mentioned here combine the incarnation, baptism and crucifixion, as the means by which the Father planned the redemption of humankind. God himself bears witness to those factors, and the threefold testimony is true (5: 9). The 'water' seems to refer to the baptism of Jesus at the beginning of his ministry, which is a model for all believers. The 'blood' is obviously the atoning substitutionary sacrifice of Christ on Calvary (1 John 2: 2), who paid the paid the penalty in full, by dealing with sin, Satan, disease and death (1 John 3: 7-8). The 'Spirit' is the Holy Spirit who confirms the 'working of God' in order to complete the salvation story. It is equally true, that Father, Son and Holy Spirit co-operated to honour each other to substantiate the glory of salvation in Christ. The benefit of the testimony is the blessing of life – "for everyone born of God overcomes the world, even our faith. Who is it that has overcome the world? Only he who believes, that Jesus is the Son of God" (1 John 5: 4-5). This remarkable statement by the apostle John is similar to the one he made when writing the Gospel of John: "Jesus did many other miraculous signs in the presence of the disciples, which are not recorded in this book. But these are written that you may believe that Jesus is the Christ the Son of God, and by believing you may have life in his name" (John 20: 30-31).

Reflection

The Bible describes an era when the people of Israel had no king and, as a result, 'everyone did that which was right in their own eyes.' We live in a time of similar moral relativism – the politicians, the bankers, the police, the knife-crime culture, and the snowflake generation highlight a state of spiritual loss. 1500 hundred years ago an African born between the Mediterranean and the Sahara, was a man whose vision of God brought a change in society. St. Augustine's life is a testimony to the grace of God. As a young man he travelled to Carthage to study and found himself thrust into a 'cauldron of lust.' He was an outstanding student but found himself drowning in 'vice' and fathered a child. He was, at that time, 'a man without restraint.' When he moved to Milan to be a professor, he met Ambrose, a Bishop who impressed him with his preaching and was soon challenged by the Gospel. He began to realise that there was a cost to following Christ – and a huge storm took place as the tears flowed. At that moment he heard a child's voice, 'take it and read it,' and he picked up a Bible and read: "not in sexual immorality ... not in anger or jealousy. Rather put on the Lord Jesus Christ" (Rom. 13: 14). He found Christ and became the great 'apologist' of the Christian faith. He went for ordination and celebrated by having a party for the poor. When people find Christ they find a life worth living. (R.M. Renwick, The Story of the Church, 1959, IVF, 57-58)

The Pre-eminent Christ (1 Peter 3: 18-22)

1 Peter was written by the apostle Peter to the churches in the Roman provinces bordering Europe, what we now know as Turkey. He opened his Letter with a glorious passage of the gospel of the resurrection of Christ. It is a berakah, a Hebrew thanksgiving of praise, 'to the God and Father of our Lord Jesus Christ' who has 'given us new birth into a living hope,' leading to 'the salvation of your souls' (1: 3-9). Almost immediately, Peter pinpoints that a feature of their

lifestyle was to face up to a hostile environment, just because they were Christians. The kingdom communities are given guidance on how to cope positively, by giving courageous witness for Christ, recalling how he himself gave witness to the powers of darkness and evil (3: 13-17). The early Christians, unlike many modern believers, really believed in the existence of spiritual and Satanic powers, through which persecution was initiated. Such powers were not and are not, some mythical fantasy, for superhuman evil power exists. The apostle had declared on a previous occasion, "how God anointed Jesus of Nazareth with the Holy Spirit and power, and how he went about doing good and healing all who were under the power of the devil, because God was with him" (Acts 10: 38). Throughout this letter Peter insists that believers should take the lead from Jesus, bear testimony to his transcendent authority, and overcome, through him, the assaults of evil on the people of God.

The main passage contains teaching that has been openly debated since the day Peter wrote his letter. The passage is 1 Peter 3: 18-22, which has been divided into nine areas:

- Christ died for sins once for all
- He was put to death in the body
- He was made alive in the Spirit
- He preached to spirits in prison
- Noah's people were saved by water
- Water symbolises baptism
- Baptism pledges a good conscience
- It saves believers by the resurrection of Jesus Christ
- Christ is in heaven at God's right hand.

In order to analyse a passage like this, one commentator sought out to have a meaningful understanding of Peter's teaching. He did this by using the following adverbs: what, when, who, why and where (N. Hillyer, 1 Peter and Jude, P & H, 113). It is however, probably better to view the passage from a wider perspective rather than loose the wood in the trees!

The Suffering and Victorious Christ (3: 18)

In the letter this passage takes centre stage:

> "For Christ died for sins once for all, the righteous for the unrighteous, to bring you to God. He was put to death in the body but made a live in the Spirit."

This categorical statement by Peter affirms that Christ, the Messiah-King, died once physically on Golgotha cross. His body (Gk: sarx – flesh) expired and Christ shouted, 'It's finished' (Gk: tetalestai) and 'gave up his spirit' (John 19: 30) – it is over – ended, complete. Like a painting or a piece of art – finite, over, finished. This was a 'God moment' in that the Father, though fully aware of Calvary, let his Son die the death of deaths, in keeping with prophetic announcements (Isa. 53: 5-7). The death he died was a death for sins – the sins of humanity – past, present and future (Gal. 1: 4). Christ's one sacrifice was sufficient to take away sin and cancel its effects, for in dying as the only righteous person in the universe, the only way of forgiveness was held out to sinful humanity. His righteousness replaced human unrighteousness which, as God's perfect lamb he took away 'the sin of the world' (John 1: 29). Jesus, having atoned for sinners, was then 'made alive by the Spirit' for Christ rose from the dead on the third day after his death (Matt. 28: 6; Acts 2: 23-24; 31-32; 1 Pet. 1: 3). Jesus, in the sealed tomb, is brought to resurrection life by the Spirit, who raises him physically from death – to life. Now, with his new glorified body, for "flesh and blood cannot inherit the kingdom of God, nor does the perishable inherit the imperishable" (1 Cor. 15: 50), he visits the disciples, the apostle Paul and over 500 followers (1 Cor. 15: 6-7; Rom. 1: 4). Jesus is alive! Jesus never raised himself from the grave. The resurrection was due entirely to the work of the third person of the Trinity. He renewed Jesus for his new work, as the High Priest at the right hand of the Father. It is clear that the work of the saving action of God was not only due to his death, but also due to his resurrection from the dead (3: 22)

Christ preaches to the spirits (3: 19-20)

> "He, that is Christ,...went and preached to the spirits in prison who disobeyed long ago when God waited patiently in the days of Noah while the ark was being built. In it only a few people, eight in all, were saved through water" (3: 19).

The details of this section, have been debated by scholars since 1 Peter became part of the Canon of the New Testament. It is commonly accepted that this incident occurred between Christ' death and resurrection. That is, between Good Friday and Easter Sunday Christ descended into the abode of the dead in Hades, where the disobedient supernatural powers were imprisoned, and preached the gospel to them. The word 'spirits' is normally linked with angels and evil beings (Acts 23: 8-9; Mark 1: 23; Luke 10: 20). There is a story of the 'fallen angels,' who seduced humankind in the days before the flood (Gen. 6: 1-4), resulting in a pronouncement by God, 'My spirit will not always strive with man, for he is mortal ...' (Gen. 6: 3). Moreover, both 2 Peter and Jude refer to the 'spirits' being kept until the day of judgement (2 Peter 2: 4; Jud 6). The question then, is what message did Christ preach? Certainly, there is no hint anywhere in the Gospels of a second chance for humans or evil spirits. The message of Christ, in the light of his Gospel ministry, was that the cross and the resurrection had been vindicated by God; thereby providing salvation to a lost world. As Christ is Lord – Lord of all – the evil spirits who corrupted the people of Noah's day have lost and faced God's judgment. The Lord's supernatural powers are greater than the powers of the imprisoned spirits. As Christ is victorious there is no need for believers, facing constant assaults, both human and inhuman, to worry about evil spiritual powers who are powerless in the face of God's overarching sovereign authority (Matt. 28: 18).

Baptism and the Triumphant Christ (3: 20-22)

In Genesis, the story of the flood centres on the fact that of the then population, only eight people were saved by water:

"and this water symbolises baptism that now saves you also – not the removal of dirt from the body but the pledge of a good conscience toward God" (3: 20-21).

The story of Noah, a preacher of righteousness, with the ark and the flood, is introduced by Peter, to show that eight people were saved. The vast majority of people ignored the prophet, because 'the earth was corrupt in God's sight and full of violence' (Gen. 6: 11). Peter links Noah's family to the people at the time of the flood and to the people in his own time. The flood is likened to the water of baptism, and the salvation of Noah's family equals the spiritual salvation of believers. The water used in baptism is not holy nor magical in any way, nor does water by itself confer salvation. To underscore what the apostle means, he insists that baptism does not remove 'dirt from the body' because baptism speaks of inner spiritual renewal. Peter himself, as with the other apostles, insisted that repentance, baptism in water (implied), the forgiveness of sins and the gift of the Holy Spirit (Acts 2: 38) were the means of salvation. The phrase 'baptism now saves you' has led to many discussions as to what was actually meant by the apostle. What he is stressing is the fact that when a person comes to the baptismal water, he is seeking salvation through faith in Jesus Christ. Baptism is an outward expression, for a person is already saved by being regenerated by the Spirit, based on the work of Christ on the cross and his resurrection from the tomb. Water baptism, which in the New Testament is only for believers by immersion, expresses 'a pledge of a good conscience towards God' (3: 21). This could infer some kind of solemn undertaking toward God - a commitment to live the resurrection lifestyle. The pledge could be a petition or an appeal or a prayer to live in the fullness of the Spirit, for the Spirit plays an active part in baptism (Acts 2: 4; 11; Gal. 2: 20).

"It saves by the resurrection of Jesus Christ, who has gone into heaven and is at God's right hand – with angels, authorities and powers in submission to him" (3: 21-22). The Christians in Asia constantly faced harassment and persecution for their faith, so Peter points to Christ – the suffering Messiah-King. He is presented as a model to follow, therefore, 'in your heart set apart Christ as Lord … '(3: 15). They are encouraged to be bold in their faith, recall their baptism, for it is about dying and rising in Christ (Col. 2: 12). Furthermore, this same Jesus, having ascended to the Father in glory is now seated at God's right hand – along with the hosts of heaven, be they angels or others – for all the authority in heaven and earth is subject to Christ. The heavenly scene is a call for Christians to keep their eyes upward, and remember that Christ is in charge of all the powers that are his to use for the blessing of the people of God on earth. Everything in heaven and on earth is subject to Christ, for he was triumphant at the cross, in the resurrection, and has been vindicated by his Father. If life is tough and hard, they are to recall that they were not only 'baptised into Christ,' they have life that is full of God's persevering grace:

> "But rejoice, do not be surprised that you participate in the sufferings of Christ, so that you may be overjoyed when his glory is revealed" (1 Pet. 4: 13). Glory to God!

Baptism – New Life in Christ (Romans 6: 1-11)

The letter of Paul to the Roman church is one of the most profound documents in the New Testament. Romans' is the most organised of Paul's letters and its importance cannot be exaggerated. Martin Luther described it as 'the chief part of the New Testament, and the perfect gospel.' The apostle introduces his writing with a statement of intent:

> "I am not ashamed of the gospel of Christ: it is the power of God for salvation to everyone who has faith ... for in it the righteousness of God is revealed ..." (Rom. 1: 16-17 RSV).

Righteousness is the sin qua non for Paul, as he builds a foundation of truth throughout his letter. In terms of salvation, he presents the Christian message as *Christ for us* and the Christian life as *Christ in us*. The first is about the need for redemption, the second covers God's redeeming plan for us. He states that 'all have sinned and fallen short of the glory of God' (Rom. 3: 23) declaring the world of humanity (Jew and Gentile) to be condemned before God (Rom. 1: 16-3. 20). Paul then turns from condemnation to justification, whereby believers 'are justified freely by his grace through the redemption that came by Christ Jesus,' having 'been justified by faith (Rom. 3: 24; 5: 1). The assurance of salvation, through Christ, covers the whole life of a justified person – *past, present, future.*

Reflection

R. W. Dale, a well-known preacher from Birmingham, was facing a crisis of faith. It was the Saturday before Easter Sunday and, no matter how much he tried to be ready for the morning – he had nothing! Who, among preachers, have not been there? He had been walking round his study for hours and had no text or passage from the Bible for Easter morning. Eventually, he slumped in his chair, probably exhausted, wondering what he was going to say to the congregation. Despite prayer and looking at old sermons - still nothing! It was at that point that he began to meditate visually in the Easter events. He could see the cross and the empty tomb and suddenly, with a shout and jumping from his seat, he began praising God. Almost immediately, he reflected on God's act of redemption as he reflected on the 'blood sacrifice of Christ' for humankind on the first Good Friday. Moving on from the Friday, he sensed the Spirit of God leading him to a passage about the resurrection of Christ. Come Sunday morning, he was like a caged lion as he stepped forward to preach. Afterwards people commented that they had never heard such a powerful Easter message bringing salvation to the people.

The main theme of Romans 6: 1-11, is that the death and resurrection of Jesus Christ are more than historical facts, for those truths are the personal experience of believers. Those beliefs and the work of Christ on the cross, were being undermined by some Christians who argued that the more people deliberately sinned, the more grace they would receive. True in principle, but wrong in practice. To counteract such views, Paul asked: 'Shall we go on sinning so that grace may increase? By no means!' (Rom. 6: 1-2) 'Certainly not!' (GNB). 'No, we should not!' (CEV). Such an idea was anathema to the apostle, so he asks them to recall their baptism in water:

> "We died to sin: how can we live in it any longer? Or don't you know that all of us who were baptised into Christ Jesus were baptised into his death? We were buried with him through baptism into his death in order that just as Christ was raised from the dead through the glory of the Father, we too may live a new life" (Rom. 6: 2-4).

In water baptism, the Holy Spirit makes real in us the work of Christ on Calvary's cross and his resurrection from the dead. Baptism is symbolised by our identification in three ways: his death, his burial and his resurrection. When you went down into the water, you died, when you were under the water you were buried, and when you came up out of the water you rose with new life. Accordingly, 'Baptism expresses symbolically a series of acts, corresponding to the redeeming acts of God ...' (A. C. Hedlam, ICC, 157). One interesting feature of this passage is the use of the aorist tense in Greek, which denotes a single completed past act. This occurs eleven times in Romans 6: 2-10:

6: 2 we *died* to sin
6: 3 we were *buried* into his death (x 2)
6: 4 we were *buried* with him into his death
6: 4 we were *raised* up from the dead
6: 6 our old self *was* crucified with him
6: 7 it was he (Christ) who *died* 6: 8 we *died* with him
6: 9 Christ was *raised* from the dead
6: 10 He (Christ) *died* (x 2)

These verses make it clear that just as Christ died, and was raised from the dead, so in his death and resurrection every believer died to sin and rose to a new kingdom way of life (2 Cor. 5: 17). It is a worth repeating again, that **baptism is not something we do for God, it is something God does for us.** 'Baptism is more an act of deliverance, than an act of obedience' (D. Pawson, Water Baptism, Sovereign Word, 1992, p 14). Aligned with water baptism is the ministry of the Holy Spirit, who applies the benefit of the cross and the resurrection to our lives. In other words, the same life-giving Spirit that raised Jesus from the dead, is the same life-giving power that brings about transformational change in those who have confessed Christ by word and mouth (Rom. 8: 11; 10: 9-10). Significantly, baptism does not just speak about the removal of sins, but more importantly, emphasises a relationship with our Saviour – Jesus Christ. An exchange has taken place, the old self has been dealt with and a new supernatural nature has been given – people who are baptised are 'in Christ' (John 3: 7; 2 Peter 1: 3; Rom. 6: 3). Baptism has also been painted in graphic colours:

> there is a washing for there is a **cleansing** from sin;
>
> there is a funeral for there is a **death**;
> there is an open grave for there is a **resurrection**!

In other words, when Christ died, we died in him, and when Christ rose from the dead we rose in him. Paul continues in the same vain when he writes:

> "If we have been united with him like this in his death, we will certainly be united with him in his resurrection. For we know that our old self was crucified with him so that the body of sin might be done away with, that we should no longer be slaves to sin, because anyone who has died has been freed from sin" (Rom. 6: 5-7).

If we are to understand what it means to 'die to sin,' clarification is needed because there are different views among believers. There are basically two main views:

> 1st View suggests we are immune to sin because our old self was crucified

This is the view that 'death means death' thereby suggesting that believers are immune or unresponsive or insensitive to the power of sin because a dead person cannot sin! The first seems to favour Christian perfectionism which was popular among early Methodists and some holiness groups, but is out of touch with the general teaching of the

New Testament (1 John 1: 8-2: 2).

2nd View suggests that our 'sinful self' is our pre-conversion life

There is another view that the 'body of sin' or the 'sinful body' refers to the 'sinful self' which should be destroyed – that its power be cut off. This is the crucifixion of our 'old self or 'old man' – our unregenerate life – a pre-conversion life. The *second view is preferred because it is essentially about dissuasion because the phrase 'our old self was crucified' is equal to 'we died to sin' (Rom.6: 6). In a word, something has happened – a past event has taken place – when Christ was crucified on Calvary, he died for sin and with his death, our 'old flesh' was crucified with him.*

There are also two levels here, for there is **participation** with Christ through our death to sin, and by **imitation** of Christ our death to self is applied (G. R. Beasley-Murray, Baptism in the New Testament, PP, 140-141). To be united with Christ in his redemptive acts, by entering into his death and resurrection, cannot but have a catastrophic effect for the believer. The old life is put under the judgement of the cross, and that completed act allowed the new person license to live the kingdom lifestyle to the glory of God.

Throughout the passages we have examined there is a clear link between 'water and the Spirit,' that is, between believer's baptism and empowerment by the Spirit. It may appear that there is no connection between Romans 5 which refers to salvation and Romans 8 which refers to the Spirit, yet they complement each other. Romans 5 is about 'justification' and Romans 8 is about 'no condemnation' which is equivalent to justification. They are two parts of the same theological coin! Moreover, Paul connects baptism with the work of the Spirit "because through Christ Jesus the law of the Spirit of life set me free from the law of sin and death" (Rom. 8: 2). Baptism and the Spirit are about liberation– freedom. Mindful of his earlier teaching in Romans, Paul continues to connect them when he states:

> "If the Spirit of him who raised Jesus from the dead is living in you, he who raised Christ from the dead will also give life to your mortal bodies through his Spirit, who lives in you" (Rom. 8: 11).

Personally, the apostle knew firsthand what it meant experientially to enjoy the blessing of both the Spirit and believers baptism (Rom. 9: 18).

Baptism is about death and life but some believers, though confessing Christ publicly and then being baptised in water and dying the death, seem to have forgotten how to live for Christ. Baptism, however is also about how "God raised us up with Christ and seated us with Christ in the heavenly realms ..." (Eph. 2: 6). Sharing in the resurrection of Christ we have been exalted in/with Christ into the 'heavenly places' – the unseen world of spiritual reality in which Christ reigns supreme. In a word, we are sitting on thrones – places of authority! That is not fantasy but the real Christian world because Christians are 'resurrected and enthroned' people. Believer's baptism reminds us that we are called to live the resurrection life.

Reflection

Party life in Christian communities is a must because they remind us of the joy of our salvation in Christ. On a weekend away from home base a large group of young people had a party – **a resurrection party**. This arose out of the time when numbers of young people – including some unchurched – were baptised after confessing Christ publicly. The sheer joy, love and a new sense of belonging 'with their enthusiasm' began to change the culture of the local church. They were very genuine in their attitudes and declared that it was their baptism in water and in the Spirit, that motivated their intention to be what the Lord had called them to be. The outcome was, that once back in their home base, they lived the resurrection life, and brought others into the community of the church family.

There is nothing wrong with triumphalism if it is honouring to God, and some of us want to see much more of that in our local church groups. Let's be like Paul who declared: "I am not ashamed of the Gospel for it is the power of God for salvation ... "(Rom. 1: 16). Covid may have restricted our movements, and our corporate meetings, and limited us to zooms and on-line activities, but it has also left the door open for believers to think through fresh ways of being and doing church – church that is outward looking. Whatever emerges – and there are numbers of ways of being what God wants us to be – but let us again always be conscious of the call to keep to our 'core beliefs and core values' as stated in the New Testament.

PART 4
Living and Dying – Identity

In theology the Christian life can be summed up in four ways:

- ➤ There is Justification, by which we are declared righteous.
- ➤ There is Adoption, by which we are known as children of God.
- ➤ There is Sanctification, by which we pursue our spiritual growth
- ➤ There is Glorification, by which we enter the final New Age.

The present process speaks of our sanctification which someone likened to a painful encounter, which was a strange definition but it turned out he was mixing up circumcision and sanctification! Enough of that, but it is always wise to be able to know what specific words mean if we are to understand what they tell us about our on-going journey to the 'promised' land. One definition is helpful:

> 'Sanctification is a progressive work of God and that makes us more and more free from sin and like Christ in our actual lives' (W. Grudem, Systematic Theology, IVP, 1994, 746).

To that I would add that the ministry of the Holy Spirit is an essential partner who enables believers to live a Christ-like life.

Reflection

One pastor who influenced me greatly had been a missionary in Zaire, prior to returning to minister in England. He was a Word and Spirit person and a very gifted bible teacher. His style was direct and prophetic which made the bible live. Fundamentally, he believed in preaching – preaching that affected the punters, and after a Sunday service we were never the same again. He would take you into a passage of the bible, Old or New Testament, and demanded that you join him to 'hear the Word of God,' and he did and we did. No jokes, no grandstanding we were part of the event, the story – it was often blistering stuff. You came away from his ministry knowing you had been in God's presence for it was plain his ministry was under the anointing of the Spirit. To top it all, he was not a distant pastor, was full of fun, and adept at influencing young people not just by his teaching but by his lifestyle – a lifestyle that influenced young people into Christian ministry, of whom I am one of many. His approach to believers was to excite us with the expectations of a Charismatic Lord and Saviour who was magnificent, and then for us to pursue the truths we had learned from his teaching. In a word, he was determined to make sure we travelled the journey full of the Word, the Spirit and live faithfully by pursuing a discipleship lifestyle. I for one am grateful that he was my pastor for several years, and thank God for his love and pastoral care.

This part co-operates with our previous notes on Believers Water Baptism by understanding what it means to follow Jesus as the 'author and finisher' of our faith. Baptism, in and of itself is not, as stated, an end in itself but a means to an end – the end being to glorify Christ. That can only be done if believers work out 'their salvation with fear and trembling' for 'his good purpose' (Phil. 2: 12-13). Our concern is with our identity in Christ.

One notable feature in part 4 will be the similarities that appear between the previous part 3 and what is presented in this section. That is deliberate, because while believer's baptism includes similar material to sanctification, it is my firm belief that not enough attention is being given to the teaching in both sections (part 3 and 4) – thus some overlap. That fact should not in any way undermine the importance of the distinctive teaching in of both sections.

The Discipleship Phenomenon

Two words, discipleship and phenomenon, do not appear to be happy 'bed-fellows' but for me belong together as a way of looking at discipleship in a more provocative way. Take the word 'disciple' which has various meanings such as 'apprentice,' 'student,' learner,' follower,' and is obviously linked to the word 'discipline.' Discipline involves 'training,' 'drilling,' 'exercising,' 'practicing,' 'schooling,' 'correcting,' 'directing,' and is used as a means of improving a person. The word 'phenomenon' is defined as 'event,' 'happening,' 'incident,' 'wonder,' 'spectacle,' 'miracle,' which can suggest a 'one off' but may not! (The Oxford Thesaurus, BCA, 1991, 99, 327). Personally, as someone who enjoyed time in the armed forces, attended a Bible College that designed a regulated approach to study, a Theological College who offered course dynamics, and having jumped into secondary classrooms for some years – I know something of the flavour demanded of the Discipleship phenomenon. Generally, the Christian theological understanding of discipleship is distinct in its own way, though there are links between the spiritual and the practical, the rules and the freedoms.

Reflection.

> At the Bible College I attended, like military service, everything was regulated. The day went as follows: A bell rang at 7 am, registration was at 7. 30 am in the lecture hall – no exceptions. Private prayer in personal study rooms till 8. 15 am. At 8. 15 am, there was breakfast till 8. 45 am. At 9. am sharp were lectures and each lecture lasted an hour. Morning break was 11 am. Then two more lectures till lunch time at 1 pm. Three times a week after lunch all the students were required to work with the gardeners till 5 pm. The evening meal was 6-7 pm followed by study time in rooms till 9 pm and lights out at 11 pm. Everything was fine for me and enjoyable, but there was one daily issue for me. I happened to have a room under a student, a former cow hand who, in his morning prayers believed God to be deaf, and bellowed his prayers to the Almighty. For a year I had little personal prayer time in the morning, just enjoyed my 'friend's' impetuous and raucous prayer-time. It was a learning experience, and as he was a believer who was 'on fire for God,' there was no point complaining because he thought everyone should pray as he prayed!

Across England there are churches and Christian agencies who have discipleship courses of various kinds – some outstanding, others good, and some that don't fit the requirements for today's modern Christian culture. I use the word 'culture' in a Christian setting because there appears to be confusion among believers as to who we are. Christians are often seen as simply religious people who are rarely different from the rest of the secular society in which we live. That may be good, but it can also be very bad. Facts seem to support that theory, for in lifestyle there appears to be little difference between the two. Unfortunately, there are statistics from both the Church of England and the Evangelical Alliance which graphically illustrates that in areas of behaviour, believers and non-believers are not as distinct as they should be. This, again, highlights the value of having good discipleship courses – the new and the older believer, for the basic emphasis is one of being a continuous learner and follower of Christ for a lifetime. Those in the post-seventies age bracket should continue to see themselves as very much disciples of Christ – always learning. That is why realistically discipleship is a phenomenon, because it is all-age and is on-going for every believer. Some of the best disciples I have met have been in their eighties – still serving and still ablaze with God. They stand before us as mentors of the kingdom, and examples to younger believers, and declare by lifestyle that discipleship is part of the fabric of being a child of God. One important key for the importance of the call for Christians to follow Christ, is to see the link between believer's water baptism and Spirit baptism and discipleship. The risen Christ made this clear when he said:

> "All authority has been given to me in heaven and earth. Go therefore and make disciples of all nations, baptising them in the name of the Father, and the Son and the Holy Spirit, teaching them to obey. And surely I am with you always, to the very end of the age" (Matt. 28: 18-20).

Right at the centre of discipleship is the demand to reach all the nations with the gospel of God confirming their beliefs through baptism. This is wider than simply individuals coming to Christ, for there is a clear assault by Jesus here that God's chosen disciples are also to engage in disciplining nations. To disciple nations is a call that seems to have evaporated in the minds of Church leaders, but it is not only found in Matthew, but in Acts (1: 8). Belief in Christ, like discipleship, is for life for he is with every believer in every age through the ministry of the Holy Spirit.

The Call to Discipleship

The call of Jesus was final for it was a call that demanded immediate response: 'Come, follow me' Jesus said, 'and I will make you fishers of men.' At once, the Gospels tell us, they left their nets (fishermen) and followed him. For example, James and John were in a boat preparing their nets and Jesus called them, 'and immediately they left their father and followed him' (Matt. 4: 21-22). The call was decisive – no prevarication for Jesus – the four men were chosen as were the other eight. All the men were 'called men'; who were to be with him as followers, friends, disciples (Gk: mathetes), which comes from the verb 'to learn.' Jesus made it clear, 'come ... take my yoke upon you, and learn from me' (Matt. 11: 28-29). During the three years they were with Jesus, they were hearing, seeing and doing. To be a disciple was to be a participant not a spectator. What had been important to them was left behind, for they had forsaken everything to follow Jesus of Nazareth. Dietrich Bonheoffer, put it plainly when he said:

> 'When Christ calls a man, he bids him come and die.'

The German was to fulfil his own remarks when, on 9th April, 1945, he was executed by special order of Himmler at the concentration camp at Flossenberg, just days before it was liberated by the Allies (The Cost of Discipleship, SCM, 1958, 7). Bonheoffer's life and death became a firm testimony for a better future and model for people in Germany and beyond. His eyes were forever on the cross and resurrection, for it was by them that he wore the martyr's crown.

Jesus' call to those who had 'ears to hear' was to proclaim the alternative kingdom, the kingdom of God, but to enjoy the kingdom meant becoming followers of Christ. Jesus spoke of the hardness of the Way:

> "As they were walking along the road, a man said to him, 'I will follow you wherever you go,' Jesus replied, 'Foxes have holes and birds of the air have nests, but the Son of Man has

no place to lay his head.' He said to another man, 'Follow me.' But the man replied, 'Lord, let me go and bury my father.' Jesus said to him, 'Let the dead bury their own dead, but you go and proclaim the kingdom of God.' Still another said, 'I will follow you, Lord; but first let me go back and say good-by to my family.' Jesus replied, 'No one who puts his hand to the plough and looks back is fit for service in the kingdom of God'" (Luke 9: 56-62).

Three men appear on the journey with Jesus all professing to become followers – disciples, but each had an excuse for delaying the immediacy of the call. The call of God is irrevocable for it is from heaven itself, for Jesus always makes the right choice (Rom. 11: 29). Such a calling is clearly stated, "You did not choose me, but I chose you and appointed you ..." (John 15: 16). To maximise what Jesus is saying to the men, he points to a field (perhaps) with a farmer ploughing and plainly shows that a farmer who turns round while ploughing, will not keep straight lines and would not be going forward. In a word, Jesus had no time for those who would follow, but kept harking back to their past. Those kind of followers would not fit into God's kingdom.

A disciple is a follower of Jesus. She has committed herself to Christ, to walk in Christ's way, to live Christ's life and to share Christ's love with others. To be a disciple describes what every believer is under God. Paul understood this, and chose to be a 'servant of Jesus Christ, called to be an apostle, set apart for the gospel of God ...' (Rom. 1: 1). In writing to the church in Philippi, Paul also saw himself as 'an example to follow,' so 'join in imitating me ...' (3: 17). Truth is caught as well as taught. Renewed discipleship is desperately required in our time, if we are to correct the superficial atmosphere that has at last invaded the church of God. The media gives us constant doses of 'in your face' people with little depth. Sadly, the easy life has also entered the Christian community. This is nothing but the spirit of the age. Christ demands a God-empowered discipleship which takes the world by storm (Acts 1: 8). When the Spirit came upon the disciples at Pentecost, they began the greatest spiritual revolution the world has ever seen. God is determined to have Christian disciples full of life – the life of Christ, and full of the Spirit (Gal. 2: 20; Eph. 1: 13).

The Crisis in Discipleship

The Gospels tell us that to follow Jesus meant that the first disciples 'left all' they had and followed him. They felt the pain of this commitment because Peter reminded Jesus of the sacrifice they made in following the Way. The demand for all disciples, regardless of age, is to hang lose to this age and the possessions that are part of the western or developing world. The demand is to be willing to leave home, family, occupation, security – for the sake of the gospel of the kingdom for all that is required will be provided (Matt. 6: 33). The comparative affluence of many believers in the West militates against effective and radical discipleship. The world is increasingly deaf to a church that has sold out to materialism. It is only when the church becomes totally sold out to God that the world will sit up and take notice of what we say. The Lord may never ask us to give up everything we own, but he does want to know if he comes before everything we have:

> 'Large crowds were travelling with Jesus, and turning to them he said: "If anyone comes to me and does not hate his father and mother, his wife and children, brothers and sisters – yes, even his own life – he cannot be my disciple. Anyone who does not carry his cross and follow me cannot be my disciple" (Luke 14: 25-27).

Jesus brought to the fore all the family ties we regard as sacrosanct, and is stating that if these come first, there is no point in becoming a disciple. He has to be number one – for he is Lord of all. The secret of abandonment is obedience (Acts 5: 32), for obedience is the total response of love. A simple rhyme reminds us what we are called to consider:

> To many people Jesus is nothing
> To some people Jesus is something
> To a few people Jesus is everything

The many, the some and the few, determine where we are in relation to our heart attitude towards the Son of God. The post-resurrection story of Peter is where the rubber hits the road. The disciple had already gone through a metamorphosis, having denied Jesus three times, he was now apparently enjoying a new deeper relationship with his Lord. Then, suddenly and dramatically it all changed as Jesus, after eating with the disciples at the lakeside, asked Peter about his real relationship with him:

> "Simon, son of John, do you truly love me more than these?" "Yes, Lord, ... you know that I love you." Three times Jesus uses virtually the same question. Which really threw Simon, for he was asking how deep his love was for his Lord. It was the third time that penetrated Peter's exterior, for he said, "Lord, you know all things; you know that I love you." Peter's hurt was certainly deep but was reassured that he would 'follow Jesus' and follow Jesus he did – to his own cross (John 21: 15-23). There is no dignity about the cross, but like Peter, to follow Jesus we, like Peter have to submit to the cross.

To be a disciple means sharing Christ's life, and this includes sharing his pain, his suffering, his rejection, and his crucifixion: "I have been crucified with Christ, nevertheless, I live ... "(Gal. 2: 20;5: 24; Rom. 6: 2-8). The challenge of following Jesus is found in the words of Jesus at Caesarea Philippi: "If any man will come after me, let him deny himself and follow me" (Matt. 16: 24). In a word, when a believer is born again he is 'born crucified.' The call to every disciple is that when we deny the self-life, we can live the Christ life. It costs to be a disciple.

The Christian gospel of the kingdom of God is good news for the world of humanity. In committing himself to Christ the disciple endeavours to share Christ's love and truth with others. The disciple is called to share in witness and evangelism, "As the Father has sent me, even so I send you ... you shall be my witnesses ... to the end of the age" (John 20: 21; Acts 1: 8). To preach, speak, gossip the gospel story to people means focusing on the person and work of Christ. The message insists that there is only one way of salvation and that is through Jesus (John 14: 6; Acts 4: 12). Such a message proclaims that Jesus is the only Son of God, that he died for our sins, and that he rose physically from the dead on the first Easter Sunday. It is through his death that humankind has been reconciled to God, because Jesus paid the ransom price thereby bringing us pardon instead of punishment. It is by the cross and resurrection that there is new life and power. If there is true repentance, believing and receiving – there is new life (John 3:16; Eph. 2: 1-10). One of the great conversion stories – stories I heard many times through my Methodist friends – was the conversion of John Wesley:

> In his diary he wrote: 'On 24th May, 1738, I went to a society in Aldersgate Street, London, where one was reading from the preface to Luther's Epistle to the Romans. About 8.45 pm, while describing the change God works in the heart through faith in Christ, I felt my heart strangely warmed. I felt I did trust in Christ for my salvation; and an assurance was given to me that he had taken away my sins, even mine, and saved me from the law of sin and death' (The Burning Heart, A. Skevington Wood, 1967, TPP, 59).

Wesley's aborted mission is Savannah, Georgia, had nearly destroyed him, but through his friendship with Peter Bohler, a Moravian missionary, he survived. Wesley was never the same again after Aldersgate Street. The fire of God, through the Spirit, ignited Wesley's heart and, having been to Calvary, became an ardent evangelist. In fifty years he travelled 250,000 miles, mostly on horseback, preached at huge open-air meetings; saw countless people come to Christ from every walk of life. People would come under conviction, fall over, cry out and time and again signs and wonders would take place. He preached the Word and as he did so the Spirit fell on the people, for his style was that of a charismatic ambassador. Evangelism then, is the presentation of the claims of Christ, in the power of the Spirit, to a world in need, by a church in love. It is the privilege and responsibility of every disciple to make other disciples. (The Story of the Church, A. M. Renwick. 1958, IVF, 167).

A Declaration – Our Identification with Christ

Reflection

During the civil war in the United States between the North and the South, George Watt was drawn by lot to go to fight at the front of the battle. He had a wife and six children! A young man, Richard Pratt offered to go into battle in his place. He was accepted and joined the ranks of Watts' battalion, bearing his name. Pratt was killed in action. The authorities tried to call George Watt into the Unionist army. He protested, entered a plea insisting that he had died in the person of Watt. He requested that the authorities consult their own army records, to the effect that he had died in identification with Pratt, his substitute. Watt was exempted from further service, because he had died in the person of his representative. This simple factual story, addresses the truth of identification as presented through our baptism into Christ.

The apostle Paul, writing in Roman's, refers to Christ's death for us (5: 1-20), and then speaks of our death with Christ (Rom. 6: 3-4). The principle is that those baptised in water, identify with Christ in his suffering and resurrection. The apostle says in effect: 'Surely you must recognise that your baptism symbolised your identification with Christ in three respects: with his death, his burial, and his resurrection. When you go down in the water you accept death, when you go down under it, you accept burial; and when you emerge from it, you accept life.'

Paul refuses to abandon the ideas of Christian identification with Christ in their baptism. He is aware of the symbolism of believer's baptism in water, for he refers to this in several places (Gal. 2: 20; 3: 27; Co. 2: 12). There is also a hymn which may or may not be Paul's:

> "Here is a truth worth saying,
>
> If we die with him, we will also reign with him;

> If we endure, we will also reign with him.
>
> If we disown him, he will also disown us;
>
> If we are faithless, he will remain faithful,
> for he cannot disown himself" (2 Tim. 2: 11-13).

Many commentators see the hymn as a baptismal or martyrdom song, though there is doubt about this last suggestion. Whether it was sung at baptisms is a moot point, but true to Paul, there is this consistent commitment toward the gospel of the kingdom of God that is reflected in the lives of the people of God. The apostle gives Timothy insights into the character of God, and the character of the believer. Take the believer first. In coming to faith, in being born again into the kingdom, there is the inevitable dying and living which is pictured here (2: 11). Identification is a fundamental prophetic declaration to God, and to the witnesses, when believers are baptised in water, to the praise of God's glory. To endure, to persevere is to establish a firm way of living the dream of being a priest – a priest who reigns (1 Pet. 2: 9). Reigning in life is not just for some far off tomorrow, it is for the present as well as for the future. (Rev. 1: 6). Disowning the Lord and being faithless is counter-productive to enjoying the blessing of God, and dividends will have to be paid. The Father, through the Spirit, by the grace of Christ, will demonstrate his own integrity by taking steps to return the prodigal from denial, and will reset the believer onto the right path. He will maintain his faithful pursuit for any Christian so damaged, and will remain faithful come what may. Should any believer frustrate the purposes of God continually, which includes denial and living unfaithfully, there will be a day of reckoning, for God is never deceived and refuses to be mocked (Gal. 6: 7). God the Father cannot dismiss such behaviour, and will not repudiate himself.

Reflection

In the 1990's, as Romania began to recover from the appalling communist regime under Nicolae Ceausescu, new stories began to circulate in the press of the terrible conditions in the State orphanages across the nation. Our school staff and students based in Hertfordshire, decided to alleviate the suffering of the children. We challenged everyone to buy tinned baby foods that could be taken into the children's homes in Romania. Other schools heard about our attempt to offer support, and joined in. By the end of our food calls, after a couple of weeks, we had several hundred thousand tins of baby food. Transportation was the next question, but quite remarkably one of our staff member's husbands worked for a European trucking company. The trucking company heard about our charity approach and provided trucks and men to transport the food across Europe for free, and gave the drivers seven days off their normal schedule. The male drivers drove the trucks to Romania, arriving early with the Romanian staff waiting watchfully for their arrival. Before unpacking the food the men went into the homes to see the children, ranging from babies to teenagers. When the men saw the state of the homes, and the conditions of the children, they were so shocked – many of them wept! After unpacking the tins of food, the men had a joint meeting among themselves, and to a man decided to return on another date to decorate, paint and give the 2,000-3,000 children toys. The men were tough family men who, seeing what could be done returned some three months later with all they needed for the homes, and blessed the children with gifts. The un-churched men had become an army of carers, and the children, some of whom were physically and mentally challenged showered the men with their love. One of the men told me, after the trip, he had become a changed man. This was a 'gospel' moment for the orphans and the men. Amazingly, their company had again offered the trucks at no charge to the men but to compensate the men took holiday time to go back to Romania. This is all about identification – identifying with those in desperate need.

Believers' baptism is an outward sign of an inward spiritual work by the Holy Spirit. Taking it a stage further, in baptism our identification is with the cross and resurrection. In fact, what many of the baptised will confirm, this public act enables believers to experience figuratively what Christ himself went through. In a profound way believers signify they have died to sin, and are now living the resurrection lifestyle in the Spirit. This means, according to Paul:

> " if the Spirit of him who raised Jesus is living in you, he who raised Jesus from the dead will also give life to your mortal bodies through the Spirit ..." (Rom. 8: 11).

Once again, it is the Holy Spirit who makes Calvary and the Empty Tomb real to us, confirming that we have been crucified and raised with Jesus. In other words, our discipleship and baptism unites the work of the cross and the work of the Spirit.

Crucifixion – Dying Daily

The cross is not the end of all our ways with God, because there is the resurrection, but the cross is fundamental to our understanding of knowing what it means to 'die' daily. The whole thrust of the teaching in the New Testament, whether in the Gospels or Letters, believers are encouraged to pursue a life 'sold out for God.' Any reading of the Sermon on the Mount makes that abundantly plain, that death, suffering and living in the kingdom of God are set out for followers of Jesus (Matt. 5: 1-7: 27). The same can be said for the writings of the apostles, Peter, John and Paul who consistently faced believers with what is required to be servants of the King (1 Pet. 1: 1-7; 1 John 2: 15-17; Phil. 3: 7-14). The radical and dynamic nature of belief demands a wholehearted response. The entry point into God's kingdom is through justification by faith (the legal side) having confessed Christ, been made righteous through Christ's righteous nature and transformed spiritually through the new birth (experience side) as found in the New Testament (Rom. 5: 1; 10: 9-10; John 3: 5-7). No sooner are believers in the kingdom they become aware that to 'walk the walk' they come under the theological banner of sanctification – a process by which believers are made holy. This process is because believers are 'being transformed into his likeness with ever increasing glory ...' (2 Cor. 3: 18). Within the Christian church there has been an unnecessary division on the way ahead for believers. There are those who are cross-centred and there are those who are Spirit-centred. Some believe firmly in 'working' out their salvation while others rest in the work of the Spirit. This is not a case of either/or but both/and. The apostle Paul, by belief and practice, combines these two approaches for he is both a man of the cross and a man of the Spirit (Rom. 5: 1-5; 8: 11- 13).

Reflection

> 'Christ calls men to carry a cross; we call them to have fun in his name. He calls them to forsake the world; we assure them that if they accept Jesus the world is their oyster. He calls them to suffer; we call them to enjoy the bourgeois comforts modern civilisation affords. He calls them to self-abnegation and death; we call them to ... become like stars in a pitiful fifth rate zodiac. He calls them to holiness; we call them to a cheap and tawdry happiness ...' (A.W. Tozer, Born After Midnight, CPI, 1959, 73).

Tozer, an apostolic and prophetic pastor, was incensed at the way Christians had been led astray by celebrity leaders, who offered a 'watered down gospel' that failed to bring about transformation. The reality was that those who professed Christ under such ministries seemed to have continued their previous way of life, prior to their supposed conversion. The superficiality of many evangelical churches is a common factor regardless of the size. There are congregations large and small who are more concerned about traditional reputations, than reaching out to destitute poverty stricken families. When Christians are active in social relationships there are considerable inescapable implications. If we are one with Christ (and we are), then through Christ we have died to sin and live for God. That is why believers need to be aggressive about rebutting the devil's enticements, and pursue a life that is obedient, Spirit-filled, and by the grace of God, live to bring 'new life' to many who are on the bread-line in today's Britain. The same applies to other Western nations. The reality for many believers is that they would benefit from understanding the nature and importance of living a sanctified life:

| sanctification | sanctification | sanctification |

Impediments	Imperatives
1st Adam	2nd Adam
People of the flesh	People of the Spirit
Works of the Flesh	Fruit of the Spirit
Old Nature	New Nature
Dead in sin	Dead to sin
Natural man	Spiritual man
Slavery	Sons and Daughters
Put off the Old person	Put on the New person
The Deeds of the body	The Mind of the Spirit
Sentence of death	Assurance of Life

The difference between the two columns is startling and shows clearly the 'attributes' believers have to pursue if they are to develop into mature followers of Christ (Eph. 4: 13-16). Our imperatives cancel out the impediments, for the first column is what we were, whereas the 2nd column is what we have become. The first is about the past, the second is about the present. The straight line may give the wrong impression because, as we all know, life has its ups and downs and that is as true of Christians as in any other form of life. Our justification (conversion) leads us immediately into our sanctification (continuation) and eventually to glorification (completion). The image of the pointed line underscores a determination to be active in reaching forward in faith through the Spirit, to what lies ahead to the glory of God.

    The apostle Paul brings together the different elements, which allow believers to recognise stages they can take to progress in their faith. He writes about being 'united with him in his death' and 'resurrection,' because the 'old self' and the 'old nature' died on the cross with Christ. This meant that 'the body of sin' is cut away, allowing believers to avoid being 'slaves to sin' simply because death means we have 'been freed from sin' (Rom. 6: 5-7). Therefore, in dying with him means we live with him, due to being 'raised from the dead' for death no longer has any claim on him. In dying for sin 'once for all,' he lives with the assurance of his resurrection life, which is shared with us (Rom. 6: 8-10). He lived to die and died to live, to bring to life those who were dead in "transgressions and sins' but

> 'because of his great love for us, God who is rich in mercy, made us alive with Christ even when we were dead in transgressions – it is by grace that we have been saved by faith" (Eph. 2: 1; 5-10).

The situation is that the Christian is united with Christ, having died with him, been buried with him and lived with him, is dead to sin – it is finished with. Yet, there is more – much more for believers have ascended with him, and are seated with him in the heavenly places (Eph. 2: 4-7). That is our status with and before Christ, but being in the body – the body of sin – means that we face temptation, and though we have a daily fight on our hands (1 Cor. 10: 13) we continue to move forward in anticipation for what is to come

Reflection

> An older Christian, having read Romans 6: 3-4, about death and life, decided to act and do something practical about 'dying for Christ.' Under a strong compulsion that he's had a very comfortable life and while thankful, did not think that his life was in keeping with the teaching of Paul and Jesus' words to the disciples about 'dying' for their faith. He decided, therefore, that every day he would have a cold bath, summer or winter, and as he was going down into the water he would loudly shout, 'Die!,' 'Die!,' 'Die!.' That became his mantra for years. For him that 'cold water baptism' reminded him that he had to die to his own fleshly appetites daily for he had confessed, that he could not live for Christ unless he was prepared to die for Christ. Extreme, maybe, but the action supported his determination to see his life in the light of Calvary which carries its own testimony. Let's hope his 'cold water death' enhanced his belief that Jesus is Lord!

Theology has often been described as abstract – and sometimes it is –

as well as being out of touch with the way believers live their lives. I dispute that, for we are forced to enter the field of theological insights by the apostle, to see the ramifications of false views that can have a devastating effect on living for Christ. The key passage: "For we know that our old self was crucified with him so that the body of sin might be done away with, that we should no longer be slaves to sin – because anyone who has died has been freed from sin' (Rom. 6: 6-7). What exactly does 'dying to sin' actually mean in practical terms? Three times Paul speaks of our death in three stages: i) our old self was crucified ii) our sinful body is doomed and iii) our death means we are no longer slaves to sin. There are two specific ways to understand what the apostle is teaching, one dangerous and one righteous:

There is the dangerous view

Some argue that our 'old nature,' or unregenerate nature, was nailed to the cross with Christ and killed. Being 'dead to sin' means believers are immune, insensitive, unresponsive, impassive and immovable to sin. This is a toxic view, for believers are left living in a make believe world, where they are unable to concede that they still occasionally sin (1 John 2: 1).

There is the righteous view

The 'body of sin' is not referring to the human body per se, rather it means that the sinful nature belongs to the body – the sinful self (Rom. 6:12). This is the crucifixion of our 'old man' (AV), our 'old self' and refers to the unregenerate life – the life we had before we were saved – our pre-conversion life (Rom. 6: 6). It is worth noting that Paul writes about 'those who belong to Christ Jesus have crucified the flesh with its passions and desires (Gal. 5: 24). However, the difference is clear, for the 1st is what Christ has done and is in the past, and the 2nd is what Christians have done and is in the present. The 1st is our identification with Christ, the 2nd is our imitation of Christ. John Stott shows the difference by stating that the 1st is a legal death – a death to the penalty of sin; the 2nd is a moral death to the power of sin. The 1st belongs to the past and is unrepeatable and the 2nd belongs to the future and is repeatable (Men Made New, IVP, 1966, 46). It is true that the word destroyed (Gk: katargethe) refers to our 'sinful self' (Rom. 6: 6) does not mean extinct, but defeated, disempowered, overthrown by something that happened on Calvary's cross. Living for Christ, demands a daily dying to sin, to self and its repeatable crucifixion.

Reflection

George Muller, a German missionary, moved to England initially through the London Missionary Society, then to a Devonian pastorate. Eventually, through the guidance of the Scriptures and the Holy Spirit, he moved to Bristol and established orphanages under the title of Muller's Homes in the 19th century. Muller was unusual in so many ways, but from his earliest beginnings in Bristol he chose to 'live by faith' and seek God to supply the financial needs for his family and five orphan homes. It was reported that he received over £1 million, without asking for a penny! The secret of his life work is found in his attitude to himself, based on the teachings of the Scriptures, the example of Jesus and the ministry of the Spirit. He wrote:

> 'There was a day when I died, utterly died, died to George Muller and his opinions, preferences, tastes and will – died to the world, its approval or censure – died to the approval or blame even of my brethren and friends – since I have only studied to show myself approved of God' (G. Muller of Bristol, A. T. Pearson, 1899, P & I, 209).

Instruments of Righteousness

In writing to the Roman churches, Paul was making contact with a community he may have only heard about, perhaps through trades people visiting other Provinces, and thereby gained some idea of the way the Christian faith was received in the city. The apostle, true to his style of writing, does cover considerable ground breaking into theological insights in his Letter and, as usual overlaps the teaching with a view to making plain what justification and sanctification really means. He applies that approach in his Roman Epistle. To review Roman 6: 8-12 is to be faced with similar guidance he provided in the earlier part of the chapter, nevertheless the fact that he did so was for the purpose of strengthening the faith of believers. In dying with Christ on Calvary and living with Christ through his resurrection, believers shared not only in his suffering but also in his supernatural lifestyle. He presents a vision of Calvary to his readers, for when he died on Golgotha his life bled on their behalf to bring them salvation. Reconciliation was made – once only - through his atoning redemptive and substitutionary death (Rom. 5: 10). Christ cannot die again, for death cannot hold him, in fact death has been defeated - it no longer has any sting, it is crushed (1 Cor. 15: 55). He hammers hope the truth that 'the death he died, he died to sin once for all' for his death was a sealing, a completion, an ending, a final moment in the history of the Cosmos. The death of death was the Father's means of rescuing and restoring humanity, as well as creation, to its rightful owner – the sovereign Lord (Rom. 8: 18-25). In line with this is the dynamic of new resurrection power for all believers are sanctioned through the supernatural work of the Spirit of God. As Christ 'lives, he lives to God' with the children of God in a new environment – the church of the kingdom (Rom. 6: 8-10).

To endorse his earlier teaching (Rom. 6: 3-5) he then makes a plea that believers should 'count ourselves dead to sin' which means that sinful behaviour no longer dominates the life of the believer. But, and it's a big but, for there is still sin! It lurks around – it is part of the darkness of the world then and now – so in anticipation he reminds us 'not to let sin reign in your mortal body' for the call is to deny 'sin's evil desires' (Rom. 6: 11-12). Blisteringly, Paul urges believers to avoid 'offering parts of your body, as instruments of wickedness,' a practical act that takes place in the mind and heart before worked out practice. It is a 'no go' for believers and churches. The alternative is vital for believers to 'offer themselves to God' having come from death to life, with the intention of offering 'parts of your body to him as instruments' for right living (Rom. 6: 13). It is really about taking an inventory of the way believers live and then looking closely at life choices and lifestyle, and making radical changes. The more radical, the more impact for the community of the kingdom but, and this is what matters, be ambitious. Deal with regular habits that undermine who you are and what you stand for. The days are short, the time is near because the end is nearer than we think (Matt. 24: 44). Christ always put everything in the setting of the 'end-times' – those eschatological certainties. The crunch is that 'sin is no longer the master' – its power has been broken – it no longer dominates, therefore there is no reason 'to let sin reign in your mortal body' (Rom. 6: 14).

Reflection

The Roman world was afflicted by the same moral diseases that afflict the modern world. Truth will out, that the three dominating areas are the same for both worlds – money, sex and power. In the history of the modern church, during and after 'times of refreshing in the Lord' a number of church leaders across the nations fell to one if not all those temptations. Some were local church leaders, but there were others with national and international reputations that 'supped at the devil's table.' That included men and women who had had outstanding teaching and charismatic ministries. The outcome of those 'losses,' even where some have been reinstated, has been so severe that many have never been allowed to recover their ministries – even after repentance and mentoring. Inevitably, the prophetic explanation of the times – great hopes for the kingdom and the immediate future of the church – has been dented and costly to the wider community. Some of the anticipated moves have never materialised, despite a panoply of aggressive kingdom prophecy, planning and longing. The Lord has not left his church, but seems to be taking a long hard look at the church in the West. Hopefully, there will be another day – a day of untold supernatural ministry – when God will release his 'Ruach' again so that the fire falls and God's glory is manifested for all to see. G. Chesteron wrote over a hundred years ago, "At least five times ... faith has to all appearances gone to the dogs. In each of the five cases it was the dog that died." There are signs of hope that God is beginning to commission a new army – let's hope it arrives quickly before the lights have gone out!

A Demonstration – Mortification and Aspiration

North East England was my home in my teens and early twenties and, because of that, the annual summer Keswick convention attracted some Christian young people, of which I was one and the convention became an annual event. The preaching and teaching made a profound impact on me. At the end of one Friday a missionary made an appeal to the congregation to consider the call of Christ for Christian ministry. I was one of several hundred who stood that day as we were prayed over for whatever God had called us into. It was at Keswick that I first heard the word 'mortification' in one of the teaching sessions. This was a new concept to me, as it was for my Christian friends who thought it sounded painful! Apart from one or two leaflets, little was said about this means of handling sinful practices. The word is mentioned in two places in the KJV:

> '... if you live after the flesh you shall die: but if through the Spirit you mortify the deeds of the body you shall live' (Rom. 8: 13). And then 'Mortify, therefore, whatever belongs to your earthly nature: sexual immorality, impurity, lust, evil desires and greed, which is idolatry ...but now you must rid yourself of all such things as these: anger, rage, malice, slander and filthy language from your lips ...' (Col. 3: 5-8).

Reflection

In 1941, Winston Churchill paid a visit to his old school in Harrow at a time when Britain was being battered by the German Luftwaffe. In speaking to the students he shared the characteristics that were needed to fight the enemy:

> 'Never give in, never give in, never, never, never, in nothing great or small, large or petty; ... never give in, never yield to force, never yield to the apparently overwhelming might of the enemy' (Winston Churchill, PM (GB), October 29,1941).

The verb 'mortification' simply means to die to sin. To mortify the flesh, with its sinful desires is to crucify it. This approach is to be an adopted attitude by believers, not a temporary moment, but a constant attempt to cut out sinful practices. To be blunt it is a brutal execution and termination of sin – but does it work? Mortification is in the present continuous tense in Greek, which means Paul is speaking of a lifelong crucifixion – not a one off. Individual believers are to be active in crucifying the flesh. If the question is asked: What kind of sins are to be dealt with – there are plenty of examples in the New Testament. Bluntly, the answer is 'the misdeeds of the body which Paul mentions in Colossians 3: 5-8 (see above) but there are many more that can cause chaos to believers. To allow the 'flesh to live' will cause the Christian death, but if the 'deeds of the body' is put aside, the believer will live a more righteous life. We are 'debtors to Christ; and are under an obligation to make the right choice. The truism is, 'if you live according to the sinful nature, you will die, but if by the Spirit you put to death the deeds of the body, you will live' (Rom. 8: 13 NIV). To deal with 'fleshy,' attractions and sins by oneself is not possible, for each believer would do well to rely on the third person of the Trinity for support. Paul is adamant: we can only put the deeds of the body to one side, by the help of the Spirit. God's Spirit helps us to say 'no' to 'the world, the flesh and the devil' on a daily basis. Not only that, the apostle insists that:

> "No temptation has seized you except what is common to man. And God is faithful; he will not let you be tempted beyond what you can bear. But when you are tempted, he will also provide a way out so you can stand up under it" (1 Cor. 10: 13). John Stott makes a powerful plea against appeasement:

'Mortification (putting to death by the power of the Spirit the deeds of the body) means a ruthless rejection of all practices we know to be wrong; a daily repentance, turning from all known sins of habit, practice, association or thought; a plucking out of the eye, a cutting off of the hand or foot, if temptation comes to us through what we see or do or where we go' (Man Made New, IVF, 1966, 91).

This is more than an aspiration of the mind on the things of the Spirit, for it is a wholehearted determination to do the deed. But most people need practical help, and this may include several important steps. There are five steps that can be taken, but these can be added to:

> Step 1: Is to focus on important values that can drown out temptation:
>
> "Whatever is true, whatever is noble, whatever is right, whatever is pure, whatever is lovely, whatever is admirable – if anything of excellent or praiseworthy – think about such things (Phil. 4: 8).
>
> Step 2: Is to use the means of grace such as prayer, meditation, bible notes, and worship in the Spirit.
>
> Step 3: Is to regularly meet with a friend and be accountable to each other as well as to the Lord.
>
> Step 4: Is to be engaged in activities with others, like a charity – working with the homeless and so on.
>
> Step 5: Is to keep your eyes fixed on Jesus (Col. 3: 1-3; Heb. 12: 2; Rev. 5: 6-13).

Mortification and aspiration are in the present tense, because they can be adopted attitudes enshrined in believer's memory banks. Diligence is required to keep focus. One of the values service personnel have in institutional life is regular discipline. Those patterns are to enable the personnel to live with the sense of being on duty at all times. That really is what all believers are called to be and do for the glory of God.

Crucifixion and the Spirit

One of the dramatic scenes in the Gospels is when Jesus faced with the excruciating agonies of the cross cries out: "My God, my God, why have you forsaken me" (Matt. 27: 46; Ps. 22: 1). The apostle John does not include the cry, but includes another shout by Jesus: 'It is finished.' With that, he bowed his head and gave up his Spirit' (John 1: 30). Both were shouts to his Father, exclaiming that the redemptive work on Calvary had been completed, and both were attested to by the Spirit. In John's write-up of the incident there has been some discussion as to whether the word 'Spirit' refers to the human spirit of Jesus, or the Holy Spirit. Tom Smail argued that giving up his spirit, could equally be including the Holy Spirit with Jesus handing over the Spirit (The Giving Gift, H & S, 1988, 148). Factually, there is a bond between the cross and the Spirit (Heb. 9: 14). The writer appears to be saying that Jesus gave up his life on the cross through the Spirit. The Spirit assisted Jesus while on the cross, and on this, there is no reason to deny that for Jesus was constantly in the Spirit (John 1: 33). Jesus then, endured his sufferings with the help of the Spirit. Even the seven cries uttered by Jesus on the cross would have been led by the Spirit, since he lived constantly in the environment of the Spirit. True, the Holy Spirit performed a miracle by raising Jesus from the dead (Rom. 8:11), but this does not detract from the truth that the Spirit was with Jesus until his dying breath.

The preaching of Peter, under the anointing of the Spirit, links the cross and the resurrection (Acts 2: 14-36; 3: 13-14). Specifically, he brings more to the people referring to Pentecost as the beginning of the 'last days' – the days when God pours out his Spirit on all the people (Acts 2: 17-21) – then show the connection between the work of the Spirit and the work of Calvary:

> 'Jesus of Nazareth was a man accredited by God to you by miracles, wonders and signs, which God did among you through him, as you yourselves know. This man was handed over to you by God's set purpose and foreknowledge; and you, with the help of wicked men, put him to death by nailing him to the cross' (Acts 2: 22-23).

Peter immediately speaks of the resurrection, ascension and then finishes by stating:

> 'God has made this Jesus, whom you crucified, both Lord and Christ ... he has received from the Father the promised Holy

Spirit and has poured out what you now see and hear' (Acts 2: 22-23).

He starts with the cross and ends with the outpouring of the Spirit – Pentecost. In a word, the cross and Pentecost belong together. The death of Christ and the giving of the Spirit are part of the whole – they stand with each other. There is no gospel of the kingdom of God without these two great truths (Acts 1: 12).

To live with Christ means that we have chosen to live within sight of Calvary and Pentecost. Living a 'crucified life' is witness to being true disciples or followers of Christ but that does not mean a stoic approach to 'denying oneself.' Yes, there is a battle within ourselves, as well as with the forces is darkness, but the Spirit is a person who continues with us and works alongside us on our spiritual journey. Our flesh cannot be 'crucified' without the ministry of the Holy Spirit. Apart from the Spirit, no believer has some kind of internal power unit that will enable us to live the 'Jesus way.' The Spirit is available to help us for the "Spirit of truth ... will guide you into all the truth ... and speak only what he hears ... making it known to you" (John 16: 13-14). We need to remind ourselves:

> "we have not received the spirit of the world, but the Spirit who is from God, that we may understand what God has given us" (1 Cor. 2: 13).

It is through the Spirit that wisdom is given us to discern the good from the bad. Learning to 'walk in the Spirit' is the best solution for living the life of faith. The best way to do this is to start the day by asking the Spirit to direct the day – work, contacts, home, people – for he is the best guide. After all, the Holy Spirit is the one who makes Christ real to us, in and through us for we all need 'the mind of Christ' (1 Cor. 2: 16). As believers, we are bearers or hosts of the Holy Spirit.

Moving Forward in Faith

One of the great classics of Christian literature is the sermon of the Revd. J. C. Ryle, with the title, 'Holiness,' and though the script is in Victorian English, it is powerful stuff. The process of becoming holy (being saved) touches on the topic of sanctification, which is about living holy lives (1 Cor. 1: 10-12; 1 Peter 1: 13-15). In a word, live as Jesus lived! Sanctification is regarded as instantaneous as is justification for 'you are washed ... you are sanctified ... you are justified in the name of the Lord Jesus and by the Spirit of God' (1 Cor. 6: 11). In the passage Paul uses the Greek aorist past tense to declare that something happened to the Corinthians – they were made just and declared holy. For example, we can say:

> Justification delivers us from the penalty of sin, whereas sanctification delivers us from the power of sin. Justification has to do with our standing before God, and is instantaneous. Sanctification has to do with our character and conduct and is both instantaneous and progressive.

This is a picture of the way God sees us, bearing in mind that we are not the finished article – we are in a learning curve. The power of the Spirit without purity of character is detrimental to Christian discipleship, for both are necessary. One feature that is evident throughout the apostolic writings is the demand that believers conform to the pattern God has ordained for them (Eph. 1: 15-19; Gal. 2: 22). Hopefully, all who intend to live as disciples will resolve to act and live in a responsible way for: '... whatever you do, whether in word or deed, do it all in the name of the Lord Jesus, giving thanks to God the Father' (Col. 3: 17).

No matter how old a person's faith is, there are times when the Lord calls us into a deeper spiritual way of life. It is factually true that the Lord constantly gives to us – he is a giver – his giving to us is often overwhelming. Alongside that it is also true that he is in the renovation business, for most of us have rough edges, and he is determined to smooth down what he observes. As disciples, we are called to conform to the Father's purpose for our lives, and that purpose is to represent him before the world of humanity. The only way we can effectively do that is to be fully alive in the Spirit. However, there is one matter that often trips us up – a three letter word – sin (selfish in nature). William Temple, a former Archbishop, put it wisely: 'A great deal of attention has been given to sins as compared to sin ... for I share the common sin of mankind, and make myself ... the centre of the world.' That is the meaning of sin. Too busy doing things in our own way, for fundamentally many of us still have the tendency towards independence. The Adam and Eve story, with the tragedy of the Fall (Gen. 3), recalls us to a truth that we have a genetic disorder – our DNA is not only faulty, it dams us. The result is that our affection, conscience, memory and will have been distorted and corrupted which Paul describes as falling 'short of the glory of God' (Rom. 3: 23). The effect is that sin incriminates, separates, alienates, confirming human rebellion against God and can also destroy relationships. Strewth, as my Australian friends would say, surely not for we have been to the cross, washed in the blood and are free in Christ, so that just cannot be us – can it? Well, it is us for there are times when we are guilty of letting our 'pre-conversion life' dominate our present Christian lifestyle. I have been in too many pastoral situations with members and leaders to ignore a propensity to fall back into the 'old man' or 'old nature' syndrome.

Reflection

The HOF, a church based in Lewisham, London, with links across the nation had a strong holiness philosophy. In the course of ministering in London, I had cause to share fellowship with some of the people in their church network. They were full of spiritual language – nothing wrong with that – but they had 'coded' words for nearly every conversation was replete with set phrases. It was difficult to talk about normal everyday aspects of life. The tendency was towards superior spiritual language, but I found it tiresome even though I regarded them as godly people. There was an unreality about their community. I contrast this with Prince Mintambo, a South African evangelist, who I met at a mission's conference and who came to stay with us in the UK for a few weeks. Prince was 6'7" tall, very gangly, and a delight to have around the house – our three children (then under 11 years) thought he was so wonderful they wanted to keep him. His presence filled the house with joy and laughter, and when preaching, spoke with love and compassion in the power of the Spirit. He ministered to us in our charismatic centre and spoke of being 'a slave of Jesus Christ' even though he had lived with apartheid, which he did not mention once. The difference between the first group and Prince was that 'he walked with the Lord' and by being normally spiritual, enriched the lives of people he met. He also talked about everyday things. Prince was a Word and Spirit person who reflected Christ, and preached to thousands.

All of us, no matter who we are, need to discover afresh the love of the Father and abandon ourselves to the Father's will and ways. There are times when, due to some changes, we have reached the end of ourselves – the end of our tether – and God steps in. Suddenly, it becomes clear that the Lord is reaching out to us and wants our attention, wants to meet with us in a deeper way with his overwhelming love:

> "For this reason ... I pray that out of his glorious riches he may strengthen you with power through his Spirit in your inner being, so that Christ may dwell in your hearts through faith. And I pray that you, being rooted and established in love, may have power, together with all the saints, to grasp how wide and long and high and deep is the love of Christ, and to know this love that surpasses knowledge – that you may be filled with all the fullness of God" (Eph. 3: 14-19).

One of the Gospel stories that has always delighted me is the story of the healing of the man in and around Capernaum. Jesus had been engaged in a healing ministry in the synagogue and the community. A leper came to where Jesus was working with the people and begged him on his knees: 'If you are willing, you can make me clean.' Lepers in those days were required to wear certain clothing, ring a bell and shout, 'unclean.' The man knew, according to Temple regulations that he would never be allowed to enter the centre of worship in Jerusalem, nor the local synagogue. The religious centres were off limits to someone like him. Being a leper was a stigma, but he was determined to speak to Jesus. Hearing and seeing the man, Jesus replied, 'I am willing ... be clean!' Immediately the leprosy left him and he was cured! The key is Jesus' overwhelming compassion and love which leads him to touch the man – clean him and cure him. Though the man was asked not to spread the news of his healing, he could not stop himself, and probably ran about shouting: 'Jesus, touch me!' He 'touched me!' Full of joy, healed, restored to the community, his family and friends, he willingly shared his transformation. Jesus, even now, is always waiting for those kinds of opportunities, whether physical or spiritual, he is always looking and waiting to touch, hold, embrace, because he is full to overflowing with a shepherd heart – full of compassion.

Fellowship of the Cross

For us, there is always the possibility of a new day, a fresh encounter with the Lord through the Holy Spirit. He is always standing at the crossroads of our lives to embrace us, no matter the condition we find ourselves in. Christian prodigals are always welcome home with open arms. Some of us, would do well to return to Calvary's cross, revisit that day and recognise all that took place – the day of our reconciliation and redemption. As the hymn writers put it:

> Oh, to see the dawn of the darkest day;
>
> Christ on the road to Calvary.
>
> Tried by sinful men, torn and beaten,
>
> then nailed to a cross of wood.
>
> This, the power of the cross:
>
> Christ became sin for us.
>
> Took the blame, bore the wrath -
>
> we stand forgiven at the cross.
>
> Oh, to see my name written in the wounds,
>
> for through your suffering I am free.
>
> Death is crushed to death;
>
> life is mine to live, Won through your selfless love.
>
> This, the power of the cross: Son of God slain for us.

What love! What a cost! We stand forgiven at the cross.

(Keith Getty and Stuart Townend, 2005)

Paul used such phrases as 'I die daily,' and 'always bearing in the body the dying of the Lord Jesus' when describing his spiritual experience. Yes, he knew all about being full of the Spirit and lived in the atmosphere of the Spirit,' but adopted the 'death principle' as his rule of life.

Reflection

William Booth, the founder of the Salvation Army, when asked what was the secret of his outstanding fruitfulness as a Christian leader, he replied:

'I determined as a lad of sixteen that God was going to have all that there was of William Booth. It is not by telling people about ourselves that we demonstrate Christianity.'

Words are cheap. It is by costly, self-denying Christian practice that we show the reality of our faith.' Likewise, Jonathon Edwards, 18th century preacher stated: 'God never forces a person's will into surrender, and he never begs. He patiently waits until that person willingly yields to him. True surrender is a matter of being united together (with Jesus) in the likeness of his death (Rom. 6: 5). (Quotations: A-Z quotes)

The fire of God burned brightly in the life of the apostle Paul, for though he lived life in the Spirit, he longed to be with Christ (Phil. 1: 21) as he compared his Jewish religious background to rubbish (Phil. 3: 3-8) when compared with his new faith. Nevertheless, he hungered to 'gain Christ' for he wanted to "know Christ and the power of his resurrection and the fellowship of his sufferings, becoming like him in his death, and so, somehow, to attain the resurrection from the dead" (Phil. 3: 10). The word to 'know' in Greek is about intimate, personal knowledge for he longed to know Christ in an exhilarating way. This longing drove the apostle to want to share in Christ's resurrection, which broke

Satan's hold on sin and death. Not only that, he determined that he would share in Christ's sufferings., a suffering that is inevitable for believers, as pictured in water baptism when the baptised 'die' to the old life. Christ's sufferings and death were unique, but there are occasions when Christians are called to make the ultimate sacrifice and die for their faith.

Reflection

> Just over twenty years ago, April, 1999, two students invaded the Columbine High School in Littleton, Colorado, murdering thirteen people and injuring others. Cassie Bernall, a Christian regarded by many as 'a light for Christ' was reading her bible when two men burst into the library. One of the masked men asked, 'Do you believe in God?' She paused and then answered, 'Yes, I believe in God,' He shot her dead. Cassie didn't have much of a life, but she immediately went to be with her Lord. One December 1, 1955, Rosa Parkes, was travelling home on a bus after a hard day's work. Six white people got on and the bus driver asked her to get off the bus (in Montgomery there was segregation on public transport), but she refused. The driver called the police and she was arrested and imprisoned. She said she was prepared to die for what she believed. On 5 December, the boycott of buses began. That night, at Hope Street Baptist Church, Martin Luther King preached. In his address he spoke of Rosa Parkes, and her devotion and commitment to Jesus Christ, and of 'the iron feet of oppression.' In 1980 she became the first person to receive the Martin Luther King non-violent peace-prize. Two women, Rosa and Cassie, had one thing in common – they loved Jesus no matter how long or short their lives were.

To recap 'if anyone is in Christ he is a new creation' (2 Cor. 5: 17). Paul is full of being a new person 'for we are all God's handiwork (Gk: poema) ...' (Eph. 2: 10). God's poem is a thing of beauty. He sees a 'new creature' as a person of significance, an adopted child of the king (John

1: 12; Rev. 1: 5). In theological terms we refer to this as 'redemption lift' for God does not just save, rescue and deliver us, he does more for he makes us into a changed person. The 'new person' is of a higher order than the 1st Adam, the angels and the archangels, for the new person is a 'person in Christ.' There is within, something that will never die – eternal life – the life of God in the soul of man. The life we live re-enforces the victory Christ accomplished over the principalities and powers in the heavenly places: "Having disarmed principalities and powers, he made a public spectacle of them, triumphing over them in it" (Col. 2: 15).

As Christians, we see Christian testimonies expressed across business, politics, social action, leisure, and families – everywhere there are people who are under the authority of Christ, and because of that we have the opportunity to express the rule of God into every area of life. We are subversive change agents of the kingdom of God! Thus far, in part 4 we have looked at ways in which the cross and the Spirit play a major part in our pilgrimage. Briefly, we have considered discipleship, identification and mortification, challenges over life and death and hinted at martyrdom. Paul, in writing about the kingdom by showing the contrast between the 'everyday things of life' and a key truth that binds us together:

> "the kingdom of God is not a matter of ... but of righteousness, peace and joy in the Holy Spirit' and urges us to 'trust in him so that you may overflow with hope by the power of the Holy Spirit" (Rom. 14: 17; 15: 13).

There are two main views in the bible about the kingdom of God. There is kingdom – in our time – and every succeeding age through time until the Second Coming of Christ. Then, at the end of the Age or the End of Time, there will be the establishment of the final kingdom of God. On that Day – the Day of God – all God's children will be gathered together from the 'four corners of the earth' together with the dead in Christ to be united as one people.

> "For a great multitude that no one could count, from every nation, tribe, people and language, will stand before the throne and in front of the Lamb. They were wearing white

robes and were holding palm branches in their hands. And they cried in a loud voice: Salvation belongs to our God, who sits on the throne and to the Lamb" (Rev. 7: 9-10).

What a wonderful picture of a worshipful community celebration of Jesus, as the Lamb of God upon the throne of God. The scene accompanies the immediate transformation of the 'earthly planet' which shall be no more, for in its place will be a 'New Heaven and a New Earth' (Rev. 21: 1). What a spectacle, for at long last the first "creation itself will be liberated from its bondage to decay, and be brought into the glorious freedom of the children of God" (Rom. 8: 21). The new cosmos, and the gathered children of God will be united together –an eternal community of celebrants joining with angels and archangels to worship the King of Kings and the Lord of Lords. To which we cry, even so, "Amen, Come, Lord Jesus" (Rev. 22: 22).

End Piece

The overall title of the volume 1 is Breaking Through - Reaching Out which combine together to provide insights into the biblical, spiritual and practical issues faced by Christian communities in the United Kingdom. There has been a tendency in recent years to continue to adopt a somewhat laissez-faire attitude towards gospel work. This approach has been accentuated by the failure of many church groups to fully engage with the communities surrounding them. The result has often been platitudes of the non-aggressive type, almost apologising by doing the right thing for the wrong reasons. Cutting through all that, the question has been posed and though simple, it cuts through the jargon: 'Just what are churches there for?' And second to that, what will entice people beyond the church doors, to enter into the banquet hall? If we have a gospel that is glorious and God sent, and is attractive and all-consuming, why are the vast number of churches across the nation small and failing to attract the people. True, there is a cultural gap between the church and the world of humanity, but my understanding of the New Testament is that the nature of the church was so attractive that the church was given poplar vibes by the communities:

"They broke bread in their homes and ate together with glad and sincere hearts, praising God and enjoying the favour of all the people. And the Lord added to the number daily those who were being saved" (Acts 2: 46-47).

Two facts emerge about the church in the city:

> The people were aware of the supernatural nature of the gospel for "everyone was filled with awe, and many wonders and miraculous signs were done ..." (Acts 2: 43).
>
> The people and the message of the gospel was so attractive that people were being save daily – that is the kind of gospel we celebrate.

Therefore, it behoves the Church to move beyond the status quo, breakthrough from the church strictures in order to adapt and adopt a more New Testament kingdom attitude and reach-out to the people with the core values of the Early Christians. We have therefore, heard the *Call to Engage with believers to Live the Kingdom Lifestyle by choice.* *Thus far we have laid the foundation through the chosen topics which have been examined in Volume 1 with a view to moving forward in God:*

> **Part 1** Releasing the Kingdom - Today
>
> **Part 2** Celebrating the Spirit Spirit's ministry – in the Gospels
>
> **Part 3** Water and Spirit – a glorious Event
>
> **Part 4** Living and dying – Identity

The follow-up Volume 2 will pursue the ways in which we can fulfil the challenges of the present day. We will do so by moving forward into a biblical and spiritual approach as we return again to our core values. Above all, this will take us into the area of supernatural activity personally and corporately. The 'single missionary' is no longer a viable alternative. Teams are 'in' because prophetic evangelism is better done in teams. Jesus set the scene by 'sending out' the twelve disciples and the seventy' missionaries' and both Peter and Paul had team ministries. Yes, there were individuals, like Philip and Steven, but they were 'apostolic' in nature but both testimonies brought transformation to others (Saul and Samaria). That is why *Breaking through and Reaching Out* is still the 'catch-all' approach to moving forward with the Word, the Spirit and faith by responding to the *Call to Ignite* so that we can *Live by the Spirit*.

APPENDICES

SHAPING THE FUTURE – STOKING THE FIRE

The apostle Paul, in writing to Timothy, takes time out to encourage him to "fan into flame the gift of God" (2 Tim. 1: 6). Although controversial, the view is taken here that Paul is referring to the overwhelming experience of being anointed by the Spirit. The gift given to Timothy was "a spirit of power and love and self-discipline" (2 Tim. 1: 7). The apostle is urging his 'apprentice' to fan the gift into a burning torch in his own life – to stir it up, to fan it into flame, to allow the gift of God to recharge his ministry. Such a gift is offered to believers to fulfil the ministry they have been called upon to exercise (Luke 11: 13). This gift is none other than the gift the Father promised (Acts 1: 4) and fulfilled on the Day of Pentecost (Acts 2: 3-4). Jesus himself received this gift after being baptised by John the Baptist in the river Jordan, and the Spirit remained on him throughout his earthly physical life on earth (John 1: 33). Our Lord, having exercised his ministry in Judea for over three years; suffered under Pontius Pilate the Roman Pontiff; was crucified on a Roman cross; but rose to life when he was physically resurrected from the dead from a borrowed tomb. The forty days of resurrection for Jesus, provided him with days in which to re-enforce his teaching on the kingdom of God, until he ascended to his Father in heaven (Acts 1: 3-4). At his Ascension Jesus was received into glory, and it was from that position of authority at the right hand of the Father, that he baptised the believers in the Holy Spirit on the Jewish Festival of Pentecost (Acts 1: 10-11). That one act of the servant-King empowered the first Christians to proclaim and demonstrate the gospel of the kingdom of God. They were empowered from heaven as the Spirit fell upon them and they were never the same again – for they were embraced with an intoxicating mix of grace, love and power. The disciples had been told that when he, the Holy Spirit came, they would be overwhelmingly drenched by the Ruach of God – and they were. This empowerment was not the work of regeneration for they were already in the kingdom. The disciples were given an impartation of spiritual authority and ability by the Third Person of the Trinity. The Day of Pentecost was seismic for the disciples, for they were the first to taste the coming of the Age of the Spirit. Though the first Pentecost was unique, it was also a model or pattern for regular impartations of the Spirit for God's people. Such a view is evidenced in the history of the Church of God over the past two thousand years, and will continue to be offered to God's people until the End of the Age. As we contemplate the future there are two basic key facts which may help us to face what lies ahead in the coming years. With faith, enthusiasm, assurance, hope and desire, God's ultimate plan will be fulfilled, but this also calls on believers to 'see ahead' and it is a conviction of many that two keys are vital:

> The First Key – A hunger for God, and
>
> The Second Key – A recognition that the King Reigns.

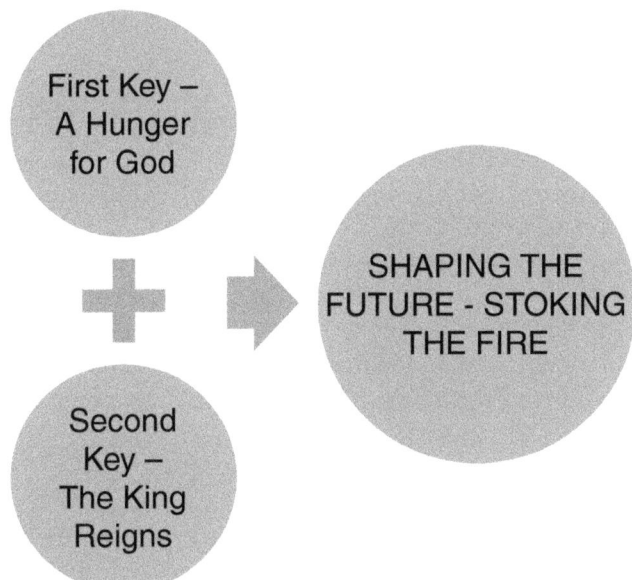

The First Key – A Hunger for God

I have been given to understand that there is a belief of a growing movement across the globe for a move of God that will be greater than the outpouring of the Spirit on the Day of Pentecost. Across the Seven

Continents, in nation after nation, spontaneous prayer hubs have appeared. The prayer hubs are not linked to or organised by any leaders, but have arisen out of a hunger for God himself. The black and Asian Christian proletariat have, after years of being largely controlled by Western leaders and churches, are coming together for the purpose of joining a global army of praying people for their nations and their people groups. Bluntly, this move has started in the developing and marginalised nations of South East Asia, the Middle East, South America and Africa – the non-white nations of the world. Latterly, the Western Church is beginning to catch up. And yes, there will be celebrity leaders who will try to grab what God is doing, but such actions will come to naught. The reason, this is God's own doing – and he will brook no interference as these hubs continue to seek God for himself, with a view to transforming people made in the image of God. Revivals and periods of spiritual renewals of the past, which stand as landmarks pointing the way forward, will bear no comparison when the Lord of Glory unleashes wave after wave of the Holy Spirit upon the Church and the world. This, in many ways, could be classed as a time before the end of time! Peter has provided us with a God-ward understanding of the future:

> "Repent, then, and turn to God, so that your sins may be wiped out, that the times of refreshing may come from the Lord, and that he may send Christ, who has been appointed for you – even Jesus. He must remain in heaven until the time comes for God to restore everything, as promised long ago ... " (Acts 3: 19-21).

And yes, I fully understand that Peter is urging his hearers to respond to the gospel like the paralysed man running amok in the Temple. In front of the thousands of the Jewish listeners, some 4,000 men did in fact believed, in accordance with Acts 2: 38. At the same time the inspired Peter pointed to another day when Jesus would return from heaven at the end of the age, bringing in the final kingdom community. Prior to that, 'times of refreshing' will come and come before the close of history – revival times.

This period will be known for its intense prayer-times due to the sequencing of these prayer hubs which will continue to make in-roads across the globe. Most start off hubs will be based in non-western nations, the western nations will emerge and follow suit – but note this – what is happening is that God is moving first across the other nations. The move of God in mainland China is a case in point, for the authorities are now allowing these local prayer gatherings to exist and be encouraged. It is not just that Western nations have become bloated in economic terms for many churches have suffered in the same way, for many key features of spiritual life have been abandoned. On-fire churches do exist in the West but they are few and far between, for the bulk of the evangelical church is still in its traditional format and is marked by decline. By and large it is the 'new church networks' that are flourishing and hopefully, they will lead the way and follow our brothers and sisters in the nations across the world.

The 2nd Key. – The King Reigns

Despite what has been said this far, this is not a sermon on the End Times, though it does reach that historical era, rather it is to take a look at a familiar prayer that is well known that the majority of Christians recite and hopefully, believe:

> "Our Father in heaven hallowed be your name, your kingdom come, your will be done, on earth as it is in heaven. Give us today our daily bread. And forgive us our debts, as we also have forgiven our debtors. And lead us not into temptation, but deliver us from the evil one, for yours is the kingdom and the power and the glory forever and ever. Amen" (Matt. 6: 9-13).

This discipleship prayer is loved by the followers of Jesus and some recite the prayer daily as a regular act of worship – though some have chosen to change the opening to 'My Father ...' because of the intimate nature of the words. This prayer comes in the middle of the famous Sermon on the Mount which in the eyes of many, is sometimes referred to an idealist picture of a kingdom lifestyle. That view is to be rejected, for it is the intention of Jesus that his disciples then, and of every age, not only say it, but believe it and do it! Here is the crunch for many of us – particularly the bit about the kingdom coming on earth as it is in heaven and by so doing fulfil God's will. The question is: Do we? Was

Jesus really serious? After all this is a prayer – a prayer to the Father – our Abba – our Heavenly Father. Some regard this last use impertinent, which is strange because our Arab Christian friends have no difficulty in addressing God as the Aramaic word Abba, because the word means 'God!' Is God then, having a game with us? Not one bit, but does that mean that we should see 'heaven on earth?' Yes, that is what he does mean. For example, when someone comes to Christ, surely that is a bit of heaven on earth? Yes, very true. Does Jesus mean more than this? Well yes, and that is where the profound meaning is often overlooked. It is true that we pray that we will do his will on earth. What does that mean? Again, it includes living the lifestyle and following Christ – come what may. There is though, another dimension that we need to look at. We have a number of important 'kingdom truths' we need to grapple with:

> "Therefore go and make disciples of all nations, baptising them in the name of the Father and of the Son, and of the Holy Spirit, and teaching them to observe everything I have commanded you" (Matt. 28: 19-20).

Wonderful, and acknowledge that this is one truth we recognise, but how does this work itself out? For many believers, there is the idea that we 'take our hats off' to what Jesus said, but that is as far as it goes. We need to recall what Jesus also said to the disciples when it came to proclaiming and demonstrating the gospel of the kingdom of God:

> "And he called to him his twelve disciples and gave them authority over unclean spirits, to cast them out, and to heal every disease and every affliction ... heal the sick, raise the dead, cleanse the lepers and cast out demons" (Matt. 10: 1, 8).

> "When Jesus called the twelve together, he gave them power and authority to drive out all demons and to cure diseases, and he sent them out to preach the kingdom of God and heal the sick ... so they went from village to village, preaching the gospel and healing people everywhere" (Matt. 9: 1).

Being Spirit enabled, they were then called upon to minister in fresh ways:

> "After this the Lord appointed seventy and sent them out two by two ... Heal the sick who are there and tell them, the kingdom of God is near you" (Luke 10: 1, 9).

The pre-resurrection ministries of the disciples were but a foretaste of what would lie ahead of them, post- resurrection. The nature of their ministry was dependent upon the physical presence of Jesus, who imparted his authority for them to be able to minister to the people. After Pentecost things changed immediately, for the promised Holy Spirit, through the Father's Promise, was imparted to the disciples to empower them for the way ahead (Acts 1: 4, 8; 2: 1-4). Time and again, the message of the kingdom of God was trumpeted and first, three thousand and then five thousand responded to the preaching. The eight thousand men and their families were supernaturally transformed for having repented, believed and baptised, their sins forgiven, and they all received the gift of the Holy Spirit (Acts 2: 38; 3; 19-26; 4: 4). In one act of grace, they were saved, being born of the Spirit and at the same time were anointed by that same Spirit. In other words, the first work of the Spirit was a matter of regeneration, whereas the second work of the Spirit was a matter of empowerment. The supernatural ministries by Jesus and the disciples, apostles and others morphed inexplicably into 'signs and wonders' as the church grew and expanded. Some critics have used Jesus' condemnation of the religious establishment by refusing to 'act out a sign,' to suggest that Jesus was against signs – but such a view is without credit (Matt. 12: 38-39). The same condemnation falls on the false 'prophets' who confused believers by performing signs and wonders, who appear to be in league with the forces of darkness, thereby insisting Jesus had the spirit of Beelzebul (Matt. 12: 24-25; 24: 44; 2 Thess. 2: 9).

The signs and wonders of Jesus in the Gospels and Acts is on another plain altogether. Factually, signs and wonders are mentioned eight times in Acts (2: 19; 22, 43, 4: 30; 5: 12; 7: 36; 8: 13; 14: 30), and twice in Paul's letters (Rom. 15: 12; 2 Cor. 12: 12) and once in Hebrews (2: 4). In the book of Acts, Peter, Stephen, Philip and Paul are mentioned as being active in the use of signs and wonders, despite the fact that two were not apostles. Beyond those references there are clearly implications to the activity of the supernatural all the way through the first thirty years of the infant Church. That is significant and supports the view of their utter dependence on God and the leading of the Spirit, as they continued to proclaim the Word (logos) of God, and the Work (erga) of God. In a word, as with Jesus in the Gospels, the first Christian's not only proclaimed the gospel, they demonstrated the gospel. Sadly, it is the 2nd part of the message of the gospel of the kingdom of God that is missing from a vast numbers of evangelical churches in Western nations, including dare I say it, in the UK. Yes, there are a growing number of churches in the UK who are involved in 'healing on the streets' but it is still a fact that too many churches do not practice what they may believe in principle. This is a negative of the churches for the people who live within the sound of the gospel – who never see it in practice. I say that as someone who lived on Tyneside for fifteen years, and during that time came across vast estates in Newcastle, Jarrow, Gateshead, South Shields, Sunderland, and so on without a gospel witness. Certainly, there was little real belief in the power of the gospel to bring about salvation and nothing about people being healed. This can be replicated across large parts of the northern shires and, where there is change – and there is – it is still small in comparison to the human needs of the people. Compare that with the numbers of Christian pastors and churches in the developing nations that have been involved in signs and wonders, and supernatural ministries for over 100 years.

Future Church, to use a well-worn concept, really springs from elements found in the New Testament Church of God. In recent years many of us have been guilty of spending time, perhaps too much time, looking at and feasting on the dynamic Jerusalem Church and its thousands of believers. While a joy, it has to be said that the church in the city was a Messianic Community as the vast majority of its people were from Judaism (Acts 2: 1-8: 3). In contrast to that is the Antioch Church (Acts 11: 19-30), which was made up of non-Jews (Gentiles) for 'a great number of people believed and turned to the Lord' (Acts 11: 21). This cross-cultural mission was an apostolic expression of Christianity. The people witnessed many miracles including conversion salvation, healing and deliverance, confirmed by Luke:

> "Now God worked unusual miracles by the hands of Paul, so even handkerchiefs or aprons were brought from his body to the sick, and the diseases left them and the evil spirits went out of them" (Acts 19: 11-12).

Glimpses of these 'unusual miracles' take place through the ministry of Paul's 'hankies and aprons' and no doubt there were other instances of unusual extraordinary works of God. When we combine the Messianic Churches and the Gentiles churches across Asia Minor and Europe, a story emerges of the global impact of the Gospel of the kingdom of God. Despite the growing persecution of the Church of God across the Empire, the impact of the 'good news' so exploded among the people, that in a few generations they had 'turned the world upside down.' One particular feature of the early Christian's was the immediacy of social care, not as an extra as today, but as a constant for we read:

> "All the believers were together and had everything in common. Selling their possessions and goods, they gave to anyone as has need" (Acts 2: 44-45). Further to that spirit "no one claimed that any of his possessions was his own, but shared everything they had" (Acts 4: 32).

Amid the supernatural ministries by the apostles and other disciples, the Church, be it Messianic or Gentile based - they adopted a principle that meant poverty was anathema, for everyone was welcomed and everyone was cared for. It is obvious when reading these brief remarks by the author of Acts that the Church was determined to give out to needy people – people on the edge of society. As they gave they hoped that people would embrace the Christian gospel of salvation and they did so in large numbers. There is a message here for all modern gospel churches, and hopefully such actions will dominate the activities of our supernatural communities quite naturally, and will be seen as a simple outflow of the gospel of grace.

Overwhelmingly, this brings us back to the core feature in our kingdom gospel and, at this point it is worth repeating what Jesus said, "Our Father, ... your kingdom come, your will be done on earth as it is in heaven" (Matt. 10: 1, 8), and they were to 'preach the message' and use their God-given authority 'to drive out evil spirits and to heal every disease and sickness" (Matt. 10: 1: 8). That is the grown up mandate of proclamation and demonstration for salvation also includes physical, mental and emotional healing. It is to be hoped that pastoral leaders and churches will engage in both. In all probability, as was said in the 1st Key, we need a spirit of revival that will motivate us to do 'the stuff' and have compassion on the next one, whatever the need. The gospel that brings new life is, in many ways, the miracle of transformation for it is still the greatest work of God for 'signs and wonders' are still part of the on-going ministry of Jesus today, through the Spirit. The call is for us to join our brothers and sisters in other nations to fulfil our wider calling and see the kingdom of God come on earth as it is in heaven – where there is no sickness, disease or evil. So if the 'sin-sick soul' is transformed, and disease and sickness is ministered to –we are seeing a taste of heaven on earth. And yes, even when there is healing, there will come a day when death stalks us, until the final days come when Jesus the Messiah reigns fully and every-lastingly. In the meantime, we would do well to live as those who submit to and announce by life and lip, that Jesus Christ is Lord, to the glory of God the Father.

Shaping the Future is a useful 'catch-all' phrase and triggers many kinds of reflective thinking related to the way we see the future as committed believers. The 'fire of God,' linked with the Holy Spirit, does need stirring, even if the embers are low, for they are to be stirred until hearts burn with fire – for fire speaks of life – and the Church, which is God's main agency, needs to be ablaze with the reality of God's life if there is to be another avalanche from heaven to earth. Given that, there was the possibility of providing different ways of doing Church, but to my mind that can be left to others. There are literally hundreds of books on such a topic, and many networks have their own 'tools' as they seek to develop the work of the kingdom through the Church of Christ. Thus far, providing two keys was a useful way of handling what are fundamental concerns for the Body of Christ. You may find the reflective keys too limited, but they do point the finger of faith at two aspects of church life that need to be addressed. The very fact that we are in a global pandemic at the moment, a truth not unknown in the Bible for Jesus referred to such when teaching the disciples (Matt. 24: 14; Luke 12: 54-59). History tells us that plagues have happened across the globe, and the present plague is simply one of many which is impacting every corner of the planet. To have such a pandemic at a time when there is constant unrest among many nations, plus secular, pluralistic, relativism, racism and political jaundice, do not offer better ways to adjust to the 'new age' of fear and frustration. The 'woke' brigade do nothing but cancel views that are unpopular in their self-centred populism, which nibbles at the edge of society and does not bode well for the future. What they failed to understand, for they are forever gazing at their own navels, is that such attitudes have been present in nations before – it did nothing then and will do nothing for society today. We are hopeful, through our belief in a sovereign God, that there will come better days ahead – for people, and for many nations. Where the gospel of the kingdom of God has taken root in the lives of many, there is every possibility of seeing God at work, to the benefit of humankind through the Holy Spirit. So we live in faith, hope and love for God's community to enlarge in both earth and heaven, to the glory of God:

> "To him who loves us and has freed us from our sins by his blood, and has made us to be a kingdom and priests to serve his God and Father - to him be glory and power forever and ever! Amen" (Rev. 1: 5-6).

We live in a world that is constantly evolving and, in social affairs that fact is clear, for there are many different worldviews. That our social views are conditioned by environment, culture, race and religious pluralism is no surprise. The 'woke' community is very much part of what some communities are, but there are also people who are viewed as 'snowflakes' because they find difficulty in coming to any strong definition of life. This, I have to say typifies generation Z or iGen. The Z generation are self-sufficient with the following characteristics:

> Ambitious
>
> Digital natives
>
> Confident

They are, given their youthful energy, people who can and do represent themselves. No doubt, there will come a day when someone will have a collective view of another new generation and designate it with a new letter of the alphabet! The key question for any 'social' generation is the same for every generation: 'Just what is life for?' The dimension in which each generation emerges, and they do change with the passing of the years, is the recognition that they are trying to find themselves. That is backed up by the 'game shows' in the media, the twitter scene, the Face-book times, Tik-Tok and whatever digital tech emerges. In a word, they all merge with the society that has developed because they are encased in the real world. The real world is what it is – the good, the bad, and the ugly. The Incarnation brought Jesus Christ into the real world of humankind and, as the Saviour of the world he came to deal with sin, Satan, disease, deception, demonization, division, disaster and death. In his three and a half years of ministry, Jesus approached people prophetically, strategically and purposefully. His central theme, right from the very beginning of his work, was the kingdom of God. By this he meant the rule and reign of a God who is alive, active, powerful and appealing for he came to serve:

> 'How beautiful on the mountains are the feet of those who bring good news, who proclaim peace, who bring good tidings, who proclaim salvation, who say ... your God reigns!' (Isa. 52: 7).

Broken down, the message of Jesus was simple, clear and plain: 'Seek first his kingdom and his righteousness, and all these things will be given to you as well' (Matt. 6: 33). The search for the kingdom was on-going for there had to be a moment of choice – for there was a call for repentance, belief, forgiveness of sin, baptism in water, and the gift of the Holy Spirit (Acts 2: 38). The call of the kingdom was set before Nicodemus, a religious leader, who was told by Jesus that he 'must be born from above' to enter the kingdom (John 3: 3, 5). The gospel of Jesus was a gospel about the goodness and love of God, for he 'so loved the world that he gave his only son, that whoever believes in him should not perish but have eternal life' (John 3: 16). In keeping with his kingdom teaching, Jesus portrayed his calling clearly:

> "The Spirit of the Lord is on me, because he has anointed me to preach the good news to the poor. He has sent me to

proclaim freedom to the prisoners and recovery of sight for the blind, to release the oppressed, to proclaim the year of the Lord's favour' (Isa. 61: 1-2; Luke 4: 18-19).

The scene was set and immediately Jesus began to preach and teach the people, and audaciously to heal the people! Without doubt Jesus was determined to 'out' Satan and his dark kingdom, by releasing people from their disease – thousands of people were healed through his ministry (Mark 1: 34, 39, 40-45). Then, to cap it all, the disciples were given the authority for he 'sent them out to preach the kingdom of God and to heal the sick ... so they set out and went from village to village, preaching the gospel and healing people everywhere' (Luke 9: 1, 6). The example of Jesus and the model the first disciples established, combines to remind us that every believer today is called to co-operate with Christ through the Holy Spirit, to offer the gospel of life to 'captive' people, which also includes the possibility of spiritual, physical, and emotional healing. Of course, as we know, there is an enemy who tries to thwart everything Jesus did then and does now and he is clearly named in the biblical record: 'The whole world is under the control of the evil one' (1 john 5: 19), and the devil or Satan, 'leads the whole world astray', from God (Rev. 12: 9). The New Testament, has many passages about Satan and his kingdom of darkness (Matt. 7: 15-20, 13: 27-28; Eph. 6: 12; 2 Cor. 11: 1-13; 1 John 4: 1-4; et al). Many references to demon activity are found in the New Testament and, according to one concordance demons are referred to seventy times. The war between the kingdom of darkness and the kingdom of God is intensifying, for this battle is not some kind of Harry Potter fantasy but a real war to end all wars. We are as much part of that, as Jesus was in his ministry:

> 'God anointed Jesus of Nazareth with the Holy Spirit and with power, who went about doing good and healing all who were oppressed by the devil ..'(Acts 10: 38 cf. 1 John 3: 8).

There are far too many Christian's who are far too comfortable with a faith that seems to be void of this demonic contagious spiritual disease. That factor alone illustrates why people continue living in spiritual darkness, for if they are 'captive people' – and they are - they are outside the kingdom of God. Jesus was adamant that only the gospel of the kingdom of God had the power to bring people from darkness to light. He explained this clearly through the apostle John:

> 'For God so loved the world that he gave his only Son, that whoever believes in him shall not perish but have eternal life. For God did not send his Son into the world to condemn the world, but to save the world through him. Whoever believes in him is not condemned, but whoever does not believe stands condemned already because he has not believed in the name of God's one and only Son. This is the verdict: Light has come into the world, but men loved darkness instead of light because their deeds were evil. Everyone who does evil hates the light, and will not come into the light for fear that his deeds will be exposed. But whoever lives by the truth comes into the light, so that it may be seen plainly that what he has done has been done through God' (3: 16-21).

In a real sense, with this as a backdrop, we are talking about 'trench warfare' for the people of God are called to be engaged in missional activity. Such warfare, if I understand it aright, is 'hand to hand' which means getting our hands dirty! Stuart Townend understood what Jesus meant when he wrote:

> With a prayer you fed the hungry,
>
> with a cry you stilled the storm;
>
> with a look You had compassion
>
> on the desperate and forlorn.
>
> with a touch you healed the leper,
>
> with a shout you raised the dead;
>
> with a word you expelled the demons,
>
> with a blessing broke the bread.
>
> (S. Townend, 2002, Mission Praise)

The way to engage in combat means joining with others in Dynamic

Prayer Ministry. No matter how we see church, and no matter what kind of network or stream we are in, the ministry of prayer is not only vital it is fundamental to the on-going work of the kingdom of God. Jesus empowered the disciples with power and authority against Satan. Christians are called to engage in the fight against the forces of darkness by praying that people be set free from any harm done to them directly or indirectly by those forces, and instead receive the healing blessings of Jesus on their lives. DPM is one of the ways made available to believers in churches or communities of faith, who engage in effective prayer for people in need. It may seem trite, but whatever the need is, Jesus is the answer. And yes, I know that is simplistic, but it is righteous. Having read many booklets and handouts on prayer ministry, I found that some were so involved that you almost needed to have academic qualifications to be able to really engage with the details that the motivation began to disappear. Yes, there are principles or ways of doing prayer ministry, and we will set them out but hopefully they will give encouragement to those who believe it right before God to so engage in such a ministry. The following 'guide' provides some clarity for those called to prayer ministry:

- All believers are called to engage in prayer on behalf of others.
- The power and authority is given by Christ to invite the Holy Spirit to come as you pray over people.
- This may take place on church property, in a home or at a conference.
- It is often better to pray in pairs if the person(s) are open to that.
- In praying for people who are not personally known it is wise to make introductions.
- Such praying is always to be done relationally for you represent the King of kings and Lord of Lords.
- Be wise, and ask the person why they have asked for or come for prayer, like a specific need.
- Listen carefully to what is said and ask the Spirit for guidance before answering.

- Not everyone who asks for prayer is articulate and may not be clear as to why they need prayer.
- If that is the case, it is wise to do a bit of prayerful prompting.
- The range of needs may be wide, so step forward faithfully, humbly and lovingly.
- Let the person tell their story and gently assist if the person stumbles over their story.
- Again, what they say is crucial and not your own story, which you may use briefly, if appropriate.
- The following list is not exhaustive: a known disease, mental disorientation, hearing issues, years of medication without recovery, cancer, fear of the future, diabetes, broken limb(s) unhealed, problems over salvation, broken relationships, divorce and re-marriage, a growth, no assurance, God doesn't love me, abortion, IVF and no pregnancy, gambling addiction, social misfit, does God care about physically impaired people, is there any hope for a sexual predator, I have been unfaithful to my partner, I want to be baptised in the Spirit, a person complains of abuse physically/emotionally, et. al.
- Whatever the need, the first thing to do is to wait and see what God is doing for he has brought the person forward for prayer and don't be shocked by anyone's confession.
- If you have particular spiritual gifts, such a tongues, prophecy, dreams, ask if there are objections.
- Laying on of hands is quite normal, but ask first if they are happy with that.
- Again, if there are large numbers present, be it in church, or a conference, give the person space.
- Make certain that you know specific verses from the Bible to assist you when praying for someone.
- If your memory fails at the precise moment you are talking with someone, use your bible.
- Don't overspend time with the person and be willing to pass them on to someone more experienced if there is a need to do that – with permission from the person you are speaking with.

- When praying – particularly for healing – some may become disoriented – and start to fall – if so gently lower them to the ground (two people) with one staying.
- Remember all that takes place is in confidence and if there is a remarkable transformation ask if the person is willing to let that be known, or willing to give testimony to what happened – no demanding.
- At the end of the prayer time encourage the person to move on with the Lord, and encourage them to 'walk in the Spirit.'
- On occasion it may be wise to suggest the person sees a 'specialist' to confirm a healing or some changes that have to take place and would value some extra pastoral support.
- Any serious matter that could involve outside authorities should be kept inviolate until there is agreement as to what might be the route to follow.
- Usually, there are pastorally trained people, women and men, present and they can be called upon when necessary.
- This is GOD'S WORK and you are the channel that the Lord, by the Spirit, is working through you so all the praise and thanks are to him alone.
- One final note – remember the Lord may pass all these 'guided' reflective ways of assisting people, because if there is a real work of God – a revival – initially none of the above will matter then – but may be useful at some later date.

In some churches and conferences people have often been trained as 'counsellors' and they are the ones responsible for seeing that the DPM takes place. At some events announcements are made from the platform that the meeting is open for everyone to pray over others, even if they have never done that previously. That approach may be of some value occasionally, but we do not believe that is the most appropriate way to minister to people. People need to be handled with care, and if that is the case, there is nothing better than 'trained' people - people who know what they are doing and why they are there – than everybody rushing around laying hands on anything that moves! Decorum is the way, for every person needs to be handled with courtesy and with wise direction under the Spirit.

On a personal note I have been party to different prayer occasions both in churches and at large conferences as one of a number of prayer-ministry colleagues. Over some forty years I have been privileged to see people transformed by the dynamic of the gospel of Christ into becoming children of God. When people are saved, born again, that is still the greatest miracle of all for needy people. At the same time there have been numbers baptised in the Spirit, cancers healed, sight restored, bones healed, evil spirits challenged and cast out, memories renewed, abuse defeated, marriages restored, abortion by women experiencing forgiveness, supported and refreshed, and children dramatically healed in front of their parents. Nevertheless, it is also true to say that I have been with people who have not been healed, with some suffering badly, some running away from God and occasionally those who have blasphemed God's name – all within church communities. I know all the arguments for and against healing, having come out of a fundamentalist church background who viewed the miraculous as having ended when the apostles died! The people believed in miracles, but reduced that to the Early Church, the Gospels and the Book of Acts. Strangely, when one of the members of the church was miraculously healed through prayer – there was only muted thanksgiving! The New Testament is crystal clear, the disciples in Jesus' day, were sent out to 'drive out all demons, and to cure diseases ... and sent them out to preach the kingdom of God (the gospel) and heal the sick' (Luke 9: 1-2). What was true for them, is true for every succeeding generation of believers for we are called to 'preach the gospel and heal the people everywhere' (Luke 9: 6), which is confirmed by our Lords' words in his Great Commission 'to make disciples, baptising them ... teaching them to obey everything I have commanded you. And surely I am with you always, to the very end of the age' (Matt. 28: 18-20).

The Foundational Basis of Dynamic Prayer Ministry

There are many elements or foundation stones that provide a basis for Dynamic Prayer Ministry, and those stones are the keys to successful ministry. Throughout his work in the Roman Palestinian Provinces, Jesus was committed to proclaiming the gospel of the kingdom of God, and also to demonstrating the goodness of God by showing the love of

God to 'sinners' and to healing the 'sick.' Full of the Holy Spirit since his water baptism and anointing in the Spirit, Jesus announced the purpose of his coming by declaring that the good news of God's kingdom had arrived (Mark 1: 15). Jesus' drive to minister to the people was his overwhelming compassion for they were like 'sheep without a shepherd' for through his 'word' of authority and his 'work' of action, many responded to him and became his followers (Mark 1: 45). There are several foundational features that lie behind and support prayer ministry. They are the givens:

> There is the Kingdom of God;
>
> There is the Person and Work of Christ;
>
> There is the Ministry of the Holy Spirit;
>
> There is the Word of God;
>
> There is the Importance of Faith;
>
> There is the Church of God.

There are other aspects of DPM which will be left for others to ponder which may or may not appear in the writings of others. My main concern here is that believing people engage in effective prayer ministry, either in private, in a hub or the home church or maybe at some Christian conference. There is one area that is fraught with difficulty and goes by the name of 'deliverance ministry' which in the past, and in recent history, has been castigated in the modern media. There are probably reasons for many Leaders to leave that well alone due to the aggressive 'treatments' some have undergone by some unaccountable networks. For many in pastoral ministry there has been a tendency to 'stay clear,' for the consequences can be damaging to individuals and to churches. I understand that, yet there are those who have significant spiritual difficulties, that call for direct Christian pastoral ministry in the Spirit. This includes some form of deliverance for those who are possessed by evil spirits, or are out of control through amoral rebellious behaviour. The best and most appropriate ministry would be to use a 'team' approach which might include a medic or counsellor through the local Christian contacts. It may then be wise to offer a series of 'prayer-times' to discern how the person is progressing. The aim, throughout ministry, is to 'carry each other's burden's, and in this way you will fulfil the law of Christ' (Gal 6: 2).

If people want to know what God is like, all they have to do is to look into the Gospels of the New Testament. The stories show a person who was fully human, but in many respects, his life ran like ours, 'from womb to tomb' (Kierkegaard). Yet he was also distinctly different, because he was the 'word made flesh' (John 1: 14). The apostle also argues, 'No one has ever seen God, but God, the one and only, who is at the Father's side, has made him known' (John 1: 18). To look at Jesus is to look at the Father-heart of God (John 14: 9). 'He is' says Paul, 'the image of the invisible God, the firstborn of all creation' (Col. 1: 15). In a word, he is fully divine as well as being fully human, and in that unity he loved, prayed, preached, taught and healed. What he did then, he still does today in his continuous compassionate ministry to captive peoples. Faced with the evil power of darkness, Jesus overcame that by dying on a cross, reconciling us to God through his shed blood. Having 'forgiven us all our sins' and making us 'alive with Christ' he 'took away' the written code – the law which we could never keep. He nailed it 'to the cross. And having disarmed the powers and authorities, he made a public spectacle of them, triumphing over them by the cross' (Col. 2: 13-15). God vindicated him by raising him from the dead, resulting in the offer of the forgiveness of sins and eternal salvation (Eph. 2: 8-10). No one should be involved in DPM who does not have a personal relationship with the Lord Jesus Christ.

Bibliography

The Day the Revolution Began, T. Wright, SPCK, 2016

Know the Truth, B. Milne, IVP, 1982

Interpreting Parables, C.L. Blomberg, IVP, 1990

A Theology of the New Testament, G.E. Ladd, 1974

In the Day of Thy Power, A. Wallis, CLC, 1956

The Kingdom of God in the Bible and Church, J. Bright, LP, 1953

The Message in Acts, J. Stott, IVP, 1990

The Lion, the Witch and the Wardrobe, C.S. Lewis, Collins, 1981

Baptism in the New Testament, G. R. Beasley-Murray, PP, 1962

The Story of the Church, M. Renwick, IVF, 1959

The Message of Romans, J. Stott, IVP, 1994

The Cost of Discipleship, D. Bonheoffer, SCM, 1958

Born After Midnight, A.W. Tozer, CPI, 1972

George Muller of Bristol, A. T. Pearson, P & I, 1899

Men Made New, J. Stott, IVP, 1966

Complete Mission Praise, Collins, 2009

Firestorm of the Lord, S. Piggin, PP, 2000

Preaching and Preachers, D. M. Lloyd-George, H & S, 1991

Spiritual Gifts, S. Storms, Regal, 2002

God Insight Out, S. Ponsonby, K, 2007

Come Holy Spirit, D. Pyches, K, 1985

Chasing the Dragon, J. Pullinger, H & S, 2006

Jesus and the Spirit, J. Dunn, SCM, 2009

Greater Works, Smith Wigglesworth, W, 1999

Systematic Theology, W. Grudem, IVP, 1994

Heavenly Man, Brother Yun, S, 2003

Turnings, G. Chevreau, S, 2004

Make Room for a Miracle, M and B Chavda, Chosen, 2009

The Sear, J. Goll, D, 2012

1 Corinthians, C. L. Blomberg, TNIVAP, 1994

1 Corinthians, G. Fee, E, 1987

Signs and Wonders Today, D. Bridge, IVF, 1985

Prophecy, T. Pain, KP, 1986

Tongues and Explanations, T. Pain, KP, 1986

Discerning Spirits, F. Frangipane, AIAP, 1991

Spirit Baptism and Tongue Speaking, Dr. I. A. Schep, FT, 1970

Fire in the Fireplace, C. E. Hummel, M, 1981

I Believe in Church Growth, E. Gibbs, H, 1981

Ephesians, A. T. Lincoln, WBP, 1990

Acts, B. Milne, CF, 2010

Redisdovering Holiness, J. I. Packer, VB, 1992

Victory over the Darkness, N. T. Anderson, M, 2005

The Gospel Driven Church, I. Stackhouse, PP, 2004

Jesus Baptises in One Holy Spirit, D. Pawson, TNP, 1997

Words, Wonders and Powers, M. Percy, SPCK, 1996

Moving in the Prophetic, G. Haslem, M, 2009

Charismatic Renewal, Smail, Walker, and Wright, SPCK, 1995

Promise and Presence, J. E. Colwell, P, 2005

Keep in Step with the Spirit, J. I. Packer, IVP, 1984

www.ingramcontent.com/pod-product-compliance
Lightning Source LLC
Chambersburg PA
CBHW041139110526
44590CB00027B/4073